'CWTCH'
The story of Wattstown

by

KEN BAKER

FIRST PUBLISHED 2003

ISBN 0 9542034 0 2

PUBLISHED BY
KEN BAKER
32 PLEASANT VIEW, WATTSTOWN, PORTH,
SOUTH WALES, CF39 0PW

DESIGNED AND PRODUCED IN WATTSTOWN
BY
GLENSIDE PRINTING

To Ynis
for all her patience
and encouragement

Acknowledgements

Grateful thanks to all those who willingly gave their time to talk, and to share their memories; to all who kindly lent their precious photographs and have been so patient.

In alphabetical order: Hugh Barrow, Mrs Batstone, Lionel Bosley, Mike Clement, Jack Collins, Trevor Collins, Pearl Dance, Lily Daniels, Ben Davies, Douglas Davies, Rosa and George Davies, Neville Davies, Evelyn Day, Edgar and Betty Evans, Geoff Evans, Gill Viner, Ken Evans, Gwenda Gough, Reg Holland, Ceinwen Howell, Mary James, Emlyn Jenkins, Megan and Haydn Jenkins, Elaine Jones, Cyril and Lynfa Jones, Mansell Kittley, Dawn Lane, Lionel Langford, Doreen Lewis, Enid Lewis, Mansel Llewelyn, Jack Lloyd, Lily Lovering, Phoebe Morgan, Robert Morris, David Owen, Phyllis Owen, Dorothy Pearce, Eben Phillips, Ray Powell, Eluned Richards, Tom Richards, Ivor Rosser, Valmai Rowlands, Byron Seldon, Linda Sparrow, Ruby Vale, Graham Williams, Madge Wiltshire.

Mr Keith Williams and the staff of Aberllechau School, the Wattstown Social Club, the staff of the reference section of Treorchy Library, and the use of the maps by courtesy of Ordnance Survey; Glyn Davies, without whom this would not be printed, and to Mary O'Brien for all the long hours spent on the manuscripts and the computer.

Introduction

✦

My first view of Wattstown was on an early October morning in 1954, from the upper deck of a Rhondda bus as it crossed the railway bridge at Danygraig Terrace. The village seemed to loom out of a mist that swirled around gas street lights and, together with heavy rain, gave me an impression of some ghastly, ghostly place to which I had come for my first job.

It was four years later that I met my wife, Ynis, whilst on holiday at the Malt House, Wick and in 1961 we came to live at 32 Pleasant View, the home of Mr & Mrs Peel.

During those forty years, Wattstown has become our home, and the village as we knew it has changed a great deal especially, it seems, since the closing of the colliery. Some of our buildings have disappeared altogether and it is this change which filled me with a sense of urgency, and prompted me to compile as much information of our past as I could.

I truly believe that it is important for every generation to know the hardships and struggles of our parents and grandparents. The need to capture the memories of the older generation is important for, in their passing, the memories will be lost for ever . . . while we continue to make history of our own lives.

It was not my intention, at the outset, to cover such a complete history as we have here, but a casual interest in some old photographs started me on an ever-widening search for the life of 'Cwtch' since its very beginnings. Please understand that I could never hope to cover every aspect, every family, or even every event that has occurred in Wattstown during the last 150 years, but I have attempted to include as much as I possibly can.

I am sure there are others in the community with photographs and memories which would add to the history of our village and until such time as these are written, I am grateful beyond measure for the help and generous assistance so kindly and readily given by all whose memories and photographs etc. have made this book possible.

1

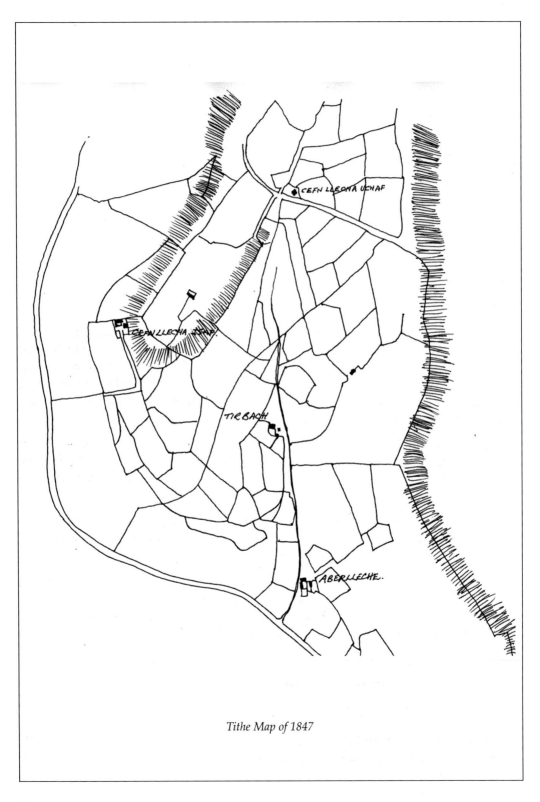

Tithe Map of 1847

Cwtch

꧁ ꧂

On the tithe map of 1847, just two farms were present in the vicinity of the modern day Wattstown. One was **Aberlleche** Farm, which gave its name to the area we know as Aberllechau Road, and which in turn took its name from the stream, **Nantellechau** that runs down into the Afon Rhondda Fach. Aberllechau describes well the point where the stream meets the river. Higher up the stream, overlooking Aberllechau, is **Ty'yr'gweydd** Farm.

This was built during the middle of the 19th century. The original farm was known as **Tir Bach** and has been in existence for centuries. Anyone who has the deeds to their house in Wattstown will find their ground was once part of Tir Bach Farm.

This ground was part of the **Crawshay Bailey** Estate. The mountainside on which these farms exist is known as **Cefn Gwyngul**. Llechau refers to 'flat stones', of which there is an abundance in the area.

However, there is another farm which cannot be omitted because of the part it played in the history of Wattstown. This is situated in the field above the 'rocks' and it was known as **Cefn Llechau Isha**. Some of our older relatives will remember it. Some of the families who lived there still remain in the area.

So we have: ABERLLECHAU FARM

TY'YR'GWEYDD FARM

CEFN LLECHAU ISHA

These were the only buildings in the area, which has long been known as 'Cwtch'. In the Ordnance Survey Map of 1873, the picture changed as the discovery of coal brought about the need for workers and transport.

Census

The earliest census in Britain took place in 1841. Those residents who were here then, lived in a place of pastoral beauty and wooded hillsides. The Llechau Woods were known for centuries and, like so much of our valleys, must have been beautiful to see, with its peaceful meadows and its river filled with trout and salmon.

The residents of the farms in 1841 were:

Aberllechau Farm			
	Isaac Lewis	aged 30 years	*farmer*
	Selina Lewis	aged 25 years	*wife*
	Evan Lewis	aged 6 years	*son*
	Catherine Lewis	aged 4 years	*daughter*
	Jan Lewis	aged 2 years	*son*
	Sarah Lewis	aged 5 months	*daughter*
	Jane Rickard	aged 20 years	*servant*

Ty Gwaudd Farm			
	Nicholas Herbert	aged 50 years	*farmer*
	Mary Herbert	aged 55 years	*wife*
	Thomas Herbert	aged 15 years	*son*
	Margaret Herbert	aged 15 years	*daughter*
	Walter Herbert	aged 12 years	*son*
	Walter Herbert	aged 80 years	*grandfather*

Cefn Llechau Isha Farm			
	Evan David	aged 55 years	*farmer*
	Gwenllian David	aged 55 years	*wife*
	John David	aged 15 years	*son*
	Elizabeth Thomas	aged 11 years	*servant*

At that time, the population consisted of families who had lived in the area for many generations. With the discovery of coal in the valleys, this would change very soon.

1861 CENSUS

The census of 1861 reveals some changes. A bridge, a wooden structure, crosses the river which forms the boundary between the parishes of Llanwynno and Ystradyfodwg. The present bridge was built by the Ystradyfodwg Board in 1884. The area becomes **Pont Rhyd y Cwch**, a translation of which refers to a bridge crossing a boat, or a boat crossing. Whatever the real meaning of the Welsh name, it was in this census that the Butcher's Arms first appears.

Also at this time, there was a railway, in existence since 1856, when it reached Ferndale.

Those who lived here then were:

Aberllechau Farm has new tenants yet again:

Lewis Evans	aged 77 years	*farmer*
Sarah Evans	aged 67 years	*wife*
Morgan Evans	aged 44 years	*son*
Thomas Evans	aged 33 years	*son*
Sarah Lewis	aged 24 years	*servant and daughter-in-law*
Sarah Evans	aged 7 years	*visitor*

Ty'r Gwaudd Farm has new tenants, too, moved up from Aberllechau Farm

Richard Evans	aged 42 years	*farmer*
Jane Evans	aged 42 years	*wife*
Catherine Evans	aged 15 years	*daughter*
Evan Evans	aged 14 years	*son*
Maria Evans	aged 11 years	*daughter*
Thomas Evans	aged 9 years	*son*
David Davies	aged 7 years	*servant*

Cefn Llechau Isha Farm

John David	aged 36 years	*farmer*
Mary David	aged 35 years	*wife*
Gwenllian David	aged 14 years	*daughter*
Mary David	aged 13 years	*daughter*
William David	aged 2 years	*son*
Margaret David	aged 4 months	*daughter*
Jacob Llewelyn	aged 50 years	*labourer*

Butcher's Arms - the first tenants:

William Lewis	Head	aged 30 years	*butcher and publican*
Mary Lewis	Wife	aged 33 years	
David Lewis	Son	aged 8 years	*scholar*
Richard Lewis	Son	aged 6 years	*scholar*

Catherine Lewis	Daughter	aged 5 years	*scholar*
Mary Lewis	Daughter	aged 2 years	*scholar*
Gwilym Lewis	Son	aged 1 year	*scholar*
Emily Lewis		aged 13 years	*servant*

It is from this period onwards that the village begins to grow, slowly at first. There are, by now, three collieries in the Rhondda Fach:

TROEDYRHIW *(Aber Rhondda)* 1854

YNYSHIR *(Jones Pit)* 1849

CYNLLWYN DU *(Pontygwaith or Tylorstown No. 8)* 1858

All this expansion in the valley, together with the increased population, meant that Pont Rhyd y Cwch was becoming a thoroughfare, if only a quiet one by today's standards.

1871 CENSUS

Aberllechau Farm:

William Herbert	Head	aged 52 years	*coalminer*
Margaret Herbert	Wife	aged 46 years	
Edward Herbert	Son	aged 20 years	*coalminer*
Walter Herbert	Son	aged 15 years	*coalminer*
Evan Herbert	Son	aged 18 years	*coalminer*
Nicholas Herbert	Son	aged 13 years	*coalminer*
Mary Herbert	Daughter	aged 12 years	*scholar*
Ann Herbert	Daughter	aged 10 years	*scholar*

(No longer farmers, this is a branch of the Herbert family who once lived in Ty'r Gwaudd Farm).

Ty'r Gwaudd Farm:

Richard Evans	Head	aged 52 years	*farmer*
Jane Evans	Wife	aged 52 years	
Catherine Evans	Daughter	aged 26 years	
Maria Evans	Daughter	aged 22 years	
Lewis Evans	Son	aged 20 years	
Thomas Evans	Son	aged 18 years	
William Morgan		aged 14 years	*servant*

(In this list there is a note to say, that '. . . the farmer cannot say what acreage he holds, for he holds Aberllechau, Ty'r Gwaudd and Cefn Llechau Farms'.)

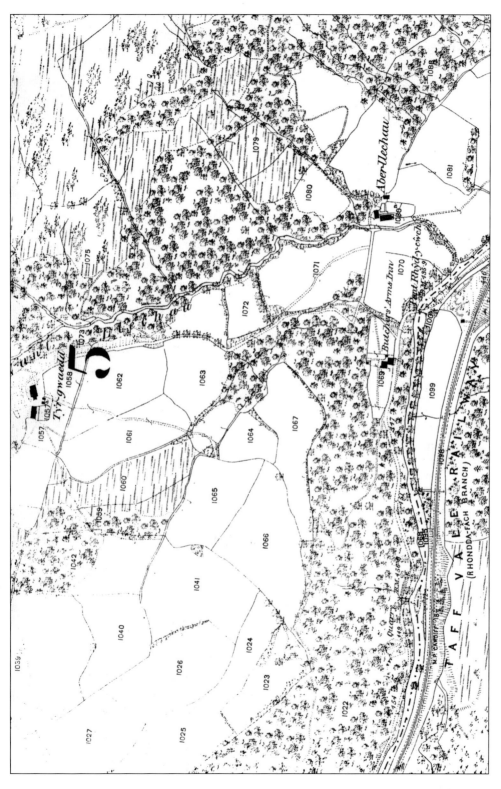

Ordnance Survey Map, 1873

8

Butcher's Arms:

Mary Lewis	Head	aged 44 years	
David Lewis	Son	aged 18 years	*butcher*
Richard Lewis	Son	aged 17 years	*butcher*
Catherine Lewis	Daughter	aged 14 years	*scholar*
John Lewis	Son	aged 9 years	*scholar*
Joseph Brownett		aged 50 years	*lodger, mason of Bristol*

(Mary and Gwilym Lewis have disappeared since the last census - William had died, Mary & Gwilym too, possibly with influenza which affected many seriously.)

Cefn Llechau Farm:

Morgan Morgan	Head	aged 56 years	*labourer*
Anne Morgan	Wife	aged 53 years	
Evan Morgan	Son	aged 21 years	*collier*

1881 CENSUS

This is the year when the 'pit' was sunk by Henry Lewis and Matthew Cope. People were arriving to live and work here, the only accommodation being at the Butcher's Arms and the five adjacent cottages. Note that these were people who sank the pit.

Butcher's Arms:

Mary Lewis	Head	aged 54 years	*widow, innkeeper*
Richard Lewis	Son	aged 26 years	*butcher*
John Lewis	Son	aged 18 years	*coalminer*
Gwenllian Thomas		aged 20 years	*general servant*
Gwenllian Jones		aged 15 years	*general servant*
William L. Williams	Grandson	aged 5 years	*scholar*
Henry King	Boarder	aged 36 years	*farm labourer*

Cottage No. 1 *(Now 35 Aberllechau Road)*

William Williams	Head	aged 26 years	*coalminer*
Catherine Williams	Wife	aged 24 years	*barmaid*
Thomas Williams	Son	aged 4 years	*scholar*
Lewis Williams	Son	aged 3 years	*scholar*
John Williams	Son	aged 9 months	
Joseph Law	Boarder	aged 44 years	*general labourer from Lancashire*
Edmund Davies	Boarder	aged 31 years	*general labourer from Monmouthshire*
Edward Beadle	Boarder	aged 52 years	*coalminer from Llanidloes*
Robert Jones	Boarder	aged 44 years	*coalminer from Cardigan*
Thomas Davies	Boarder	aged 28 years	*coalminer from Cardigan*

Cottage No. 2 *(34 Aberllechau Road)*

William Bull	Head	aged 34 years	*contractor from Sussex*
Ann Bull	Wife	aged 39 years	*from Gloucester*
Thomas Bull	Son	aged 11 years	*scholar*
Mary Bull	Daughter	aged 8 years	*scholar*
William Johnson	Boarder	aged 50 years	*general labourer from Exeter*
Charles Saunders	Boarder	aged 56 years	*general labourer from Exeter*
John Percy	Boarder	aged 43 years	*general labourer from Portsmouth*
James Vaughan	Boarder	aged 47 years	*general labourer from Lancashire*

Cottage No. 3 *(33 Aberllechau Road)*

William Jones	Head	aged 33 years	*sinker from Radnorshire*
Margaret Jones	Wife	aged 32 years	*from Montgomeryshire*
William Jones	Son	aged 13 years	*engine stoker*
Edward Jones	Son	aged 9 years	*scholar*
Richard Jones	Son	aged 7 years	*scholar*
Thomas Jones	Son	aged 5 years	*scholar*
James Jones	Son	aged 3 years	*scholar*
Abraham Jones	Son	aged 1 year	
Ann Lee		aged 14 years	*general servant*

Cottage No. 4 *(32 Aberllechau Road)*

James Lewis	Head	aged 40 years	*mason from Llanelli*
Mary Lewis	Wife	aged 36 years	
Evan Lewis	Son	aged 19 years	*mason*
Elizabeth Lewis	Daughter	aged 7 years	*scholar*
Ebenezer James	Boarder	aged 41 years	*mason from Carmarthen*
William Rowlands	Boarder	aged 60 years	*mason from Carmarthen*

Cottage No. 5 *(31 Aberllechau Road.)*

Edward Lewis	Head	aged 42 years	*carpenter*
Margaret Lewis	Wife	aged 28 years	
Llewellyn Lewis	Son	aged 22 years	*carpenter*
John Lewis	Son	aged 6 months	
John Johnson	Boarder	aged 55 years	*general labourer from Yorkshire*

Twynglywen Cottage

Edward Herbert	Head	aged 30 years	*coal miner*
Ann Herbert	Wife	aged 29 years	
Mary H. Hughes	Visitor	aged 11 years	*scholar*
John Rees	Boarder	aged 44 years	*sinker*
David Tanner	Boarder	aged 59 years	*sinker*

Aberllechau Farm - *no longer existed*

Cefn Llechau Farm - *uninhabited*

Ty'r Gweydd Farm *(Note the different spelling by the various census officers.)*

Jane Evans	Head	aged 62 years	*farmer's widow*
Evan Evans	Son	aged 32 years	*farmer*
Lewis Evans	Son	aged 28 years	*farmer*
Thomas Evans	Son	aged 26 years	*farmer*
Ann Evans		aged 22 years	*general servant*

1891 CENSUS

Now 'Cwtch' becomes a fast growing village named 'Wattstown'.

Cefn Llechau Farm - *uninhabited*

Ty'r Gwaudd Farm

Jane Evans	Head	aged 72 years	*farmer's widow*
Evan Evans	Son	aged 42 years	*farmer*
Lewis Evans	Son	aged 39 years	*farmer*
Thomas Evans	Son	aged 37 years	*farmer*
Esther Evans		aged 27 years	*general servant from Cardiganshire*
William Jenkins		aged 62 years	*farm servant from Brecknockshire*

Butcher's Arms

Mary Lewis	Head	aged 67 years	*widow, innkeeper*
Catherine Williams	Daughter	aged 35 years	*widow, barmaid*
Tom Williams	Grandson	aged 14 years	*coalminer*
Lewis Williams	Grandson	aged 3 years	*scholar*
George Williams	Grandson	aged 11 years	*scholar*
Elizabeth Williams	Granddaughter	aged 8 years	*scholar*
Catherine Williams	Granddaughter	aged 5 years	*scholar*
William Lewis	Grandson	aged 5 years	*scholar*
David Lewis	Brother	aged 65 years	*inn servant*
Elizabeth Lewis		aged 21 years	*inn servant*
Catherine William		aged 18 years	*inn servant*
Edgar Jones		aged 15 years	*visitor*

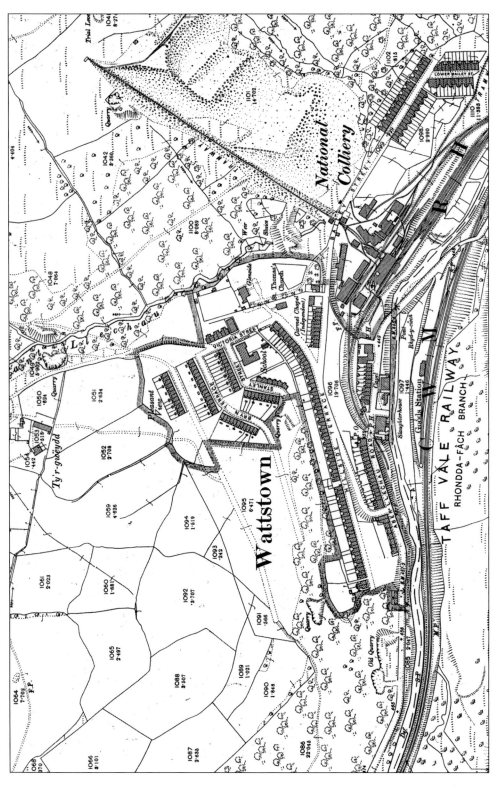

Ordnance Survey Map, 1900

12

Glenside House

James Miles	Head	aged 35 years	*colliery agent from Risca*
Mary Miles	Daughter	aged 12 years	*scholar from Risca*
William Miles	Son	aged 12 years	*scholar from Risca*
Winifred Miles	Daughter	aged 10 years	*scholar from Risca*
Gwladys Miles	Daughter	aged 3 years	*scholar from Risca*
Ivor Miles	Brother	aged 37 years	*traffic manager from Risca*
Elizabeth Tarr		aged 22 years	*general servant from Devon*

Twynglywen Cottage

Edward Herbert	Head	aged 39 years	*coal miner*
Ann Herbert	Wife	aged 38 years	
Margaret Herbert	Daughter	aged 5 years	*scholar*
Nicholas Herbert	Son	aged 4 years	*scholar*
Amy Herbert	Daughter	aged 2 years	
Mary Lewis	Niece	aged 14 years	*servant*
Thomas Jones	Boarder	aged 55 years	*labourer*

Aberllechau Road, Hillside Terrace and Bailey Street were in existence and it is interesting to see how many people lived in so few houses then. One example is 23 Hillside Terrace, with 16 people living there in 1891. They included three families, totalling 12 people and four lodgers. All of them were from Dorset or Somerset. This was quite typical when whole families came looking for work, often coming from the same district. It was people from all over Wales and the south western parts of England who made up the population of Wattstown in those days. Approximately 70% of them spoke Welsh, or both languages, at that time.

The Farms

ABERLLECHAU FARM

Aberllechau Farm, from a painting by Ken Baker

This was situated at the meeting place, or confluence, of the Llechau Stream and the river Rhondda Fach. This gave the farm its name. The valley was wider and flat at this point. The trees on the hillsides had stood for centuries, but all that remain now are the Bailey Woods and other trees scattered along the edge of the Llechau Stream, up towards Tir Gwaudd Farm. We have no positive date for when it was built, but it first appeared on the tithe map of 1847.

During the 19th century, it changed hands several times as tenant farmers moved. The land was owned by the Crawshay Bailey Estates and, in the late 1870s, the mineral rights of the land were leased to Matthew Cope and Henry Lewis, who sank the first shaft of the Cwtch colliery.

In 1884, the National Steam Coal Company purchased the colliery and it became the 'National', but never lost the name of Cwtch. The farm no longer exists, but part of the original farm remained as the stables of the colliery. This old building would have been of great interest today, but unfortunately it was demolished with the closure of the colliery in 1968/69, in spite of an attempt to save it. The farm gave its name to the school and Aberllechau Road.

CEFN LLECHAU FARM

Cefn Llechau Farm, from a drawing by Ken Baker

This was a very old and primitive farmhouse with a barn, overlooking the 'rocks' above Pontygwaith. Its age is unknown, possibly built over 250 years ago, but it was destroyed by vandals in 1947/48 when it remained empty after the nationalisation of the mines in 1947. Vandals, it seems, existed 50 years ago and are not a new phenomenon!

Among those who lived there this past century were Mr & Mrs Franklin and family (1921/1930), Mr & Mrs Owen, and in 1934/36, Mr & Mrs Hill. The farm had been a rest place for pit horses during holiday breaks, or if a horse was ill, or had been injured.

The primitive nature of the building meant that the tenants had to carry water from a well about 50 yards from the house, while the toilets were simply a moveable shed over a hole in the ground. Candles or paraffin lamps were the only lights in the house. The building was constructed of flat stones, held loosely together with mortar and whitewash on the inside. Primitive, indeed, by today's standards.

TY'R GWAUDD FARM

Ty'r Gwaudd Farmhouse, circa 2001
Built in the mid-19th century on the site of an older farmhouse known as Tir Bach

A farm has existed on this site for at least 200 years. We have no accurate record, but on the tithe map of 1847, it is named as Ty'r Bach (small house). This name appears as Tir Bach on the deeds of many of the houses of Wattstown. It was on the fields of this farm that the streets and houses were built, usually by private contractors, in groups of two or three at a time.

During the 19th century, the farm changed tenants until, in 1861, the census shows that Richard and Jane Evans came to the farm and built what today is Ty'r Gwaudd farmhouse. They remained there until early last century when Mr Walters, whose mother was a daughter of Richard and Jane Evans, took over the farm on the death of his bachelor uncles. Many of our older neighbours will remember him travelling up and down Wattstown.

Mr & Mrs Walters had three daughters, one of whom, Mari, went to teach in Czechoslovakia after taking her degree at Aberystwyth University. She returned to this country in 1939, accompanied by a young Czech refugee.

Until 1880, when the colliery took over the land of Aberllechau Farm, all the acreage of the three farms was held by Ty'r Gwaudd Farm.

The present farm appears on the ordnance survey map and, on the existing barn, there is a stone dated 1870. The original Ty'r Bach farmhouse stood in ruins in the garden of the present farm. Now only the remains of two walls exist, but it can be seen to have been a very small house indeed. Mr Walters and family remained in the farm until 1939, when they retired to Laleston. It was taken over in September 1939 by Mr & Mrs John Jenkins and family, who came from the Fforch Farm in Treorchy. Their daughter Megan, married Haydn Jenkins, who was from Penygraig. They now live in the Ty'r Gwaudd farmhouse, while their son Gareth runs the farm.

They have seen many changes in the farming industry from the early days, when horses did the work that tractors do now. They have seen a couple of their horses killed by colliery workings on the side of the 'Llechau' and many sheep killed by roaming dogs and, before the land was finally fenced off, cows wandered into Llanwynno Church, tempted by lush grass and open doors, no doubt!

During the war years, the farm land was planted with foodstuffs as part of the war effort to help feed ourselves! Now the work of the hill farmer has changed, with sheep, a few cattle and alternative methods necessary to earn a living.

The origin of the name 'Wattstown'

Wattstown received its name from a Northumberland shipowner who never lived in South Wales. Edmund Hannay Watts was born in Blyth, Northumberland in 1830, the son of Edmund Hannay Watts and Sarah Adshead. His great-grandfather, Edmund Hannay had been driven from his Scottish home in the rebellion of 1745 and had settled in Blyth, and married. One of his daughters, Mary, married a ship builder, Edward Watts, and thus began the family name that became famous for shipping and the exporting of coal.

Edmund Hannay Watts, having completed his apprenticeship in a Newcastle firm of shipbrokers and coal exporters, returned to Blyth and began his own business as merchant and shipbroker.

He soon became the owner of a considerable quantity of cargo-carrying tonnage. At 26, he went into partnership with a former school friend, William Milburn, and their enterprise and skill soon made them one of the leading shipowners in the country. They were the first company to use steamers on the London-Australia trade route.

In 1872, the company expanded their operations, and purchased the Tydraw Colliery in Blaencwm, at the top of Rhondda Fawr. In the same year, the company dissolved and the firm of Watts, Watts & Co. was established, with Edmund Hannay Watts as the senior partner.

The new firm assumed a position of great importance from the start, with extensive business interests in London, Cardiff and Newport, as coal exporters, colliery owners, colliery agents, and shipbrokers. The influence of the company extended to the control of 30 steamers, and the output of the United Collieries at Risca (Wattsville), and Wattstown. Edmund Hannay Watts died in 1902.

Early photograph of Glenside, Hillside Terrace and the School in 1888

Beginnings

⁓꠶ꞏ꠶⁓

Wattstown has its origins in the sinking of the pit, which became the National Colliery. The area has been known as 'Cwtch' for centuries and is mentioned in *The History of Llanwynno* by Glanffrwd, as early as 1790. It represents the area hidden in the valley below the Llechau. We shall probably never know the real source of its name.

In the 1870s, only the farms existed, together with the Butcher's Arms, built some time in the 1850s and named after William Lewis, the first publican, and butcher by trade.

In 1875, the first houses appeared, five of them built next to the Butcher's Arms and this was known as Ferndale Road, but was later renamed Aberllechau Road, after the farm on which the colliery was built.

In 1878, Edward Herbert, the son of William Herbert of Aberllechau Farm, purchased a plot of land and built the cottage known then as Twynglywen Cottage.

In 1881, the pit was sunk and in 1884 it was taken over by Watts, Watts & Co. They gave the village its name. This company became the National Steam Coal Company and this gave the pit the name of the National Colliery. Such was the influx of people from England and Wales, in search of work, that housing and accommodation were in great demand.

In 1884, the National Colliery Company leased land and built 60 homes in Hillside Terrace, and 39 in Bailey Street in 1885. Henry Lewis, who supervised the sinking of the pit, built Glenside in 1882-3. He occupied it until Watts, Watts became owners of the pit which when it was occupied eventually by James Miles, the agent for the company, who also gave its name to the village of Wattsville near Cross Keys.

In the 1871 census, there is mention of a Mr. Brownett, a stone mason of Bristol, lodging in the Butcher's Arms. Was he one of the early builders of Wattstown?

The first five 'new houses' built in 1875, next to the Butcher's Arms, on Aberllechau Road

Twynglywen Cottage, built by Edward Herbert in 1878

*The river bridge, built in 1884 to replace an earlier wooden structure, which gave the name
'Pont Rhyd y Cwch'*

The stone tablet in the wall of the bridge

An early view of the colliery and the original Butcher's Arms in the late 19th century.
The railway bridge is quite narrow, with a lot less traffic.

The coal tip collapse, which demolished a number of houses in Bailey Street in 1897.

The first 12 houses of Pleasant View, built in 1896

'Gorwel', built at the beginning of the 1900s for the Rev M. H. Jones and his family. Three of his daughters became teachers and Gladys Jones was head of the Aberllechau Infants School from 1944 to 1955. His son Edgar became Sir Edgar Jones.

The School was built in 1887, and Bryn Terrace, School Street and Calfaria in 1894. Next to Calfaria was a slaughterhouse, built earlier by David Lewis, the butcher who sold his meat from his shop in 26 Aberllechau Road.

The Wattstown Hotel was built in the early 1890s, followed by the first twelve houses of Pleasant View and St.Thomas's Church in 1896. Victoria Street consisted of only six houses in 1900, while the bottom three were erected in 1910 by the colliery, for their officials. By 1900, most of the village as we know it was in existence. Look at the map of 1900 to see how the 20th century brought about even more changes. Early in the 1900s, building continued with the 'New Houses' in Pleasant View, built by the colliery, while the remainder of Pleasant View was constructed by private builders, through the Wattstown Building Club, which originally started in 1896 and was restarted in 1909. The Club was an association of miners who clubbed together and, with a secretary, arranged for a number of houses to be built. Each member paid £10 or £20 down, and then monthly instalments for each share, i.e. house. When one-quarter had been paid, the Club disbanded and each householder had to pay the remaining mortgage. This down payment often took years to save. Thus, many of the houses of Pleasant View were built in 1896 and 1910/11 by private builders, leasing the land for 15 shillings per annum, and valued at £130.

1926 onwards saw the New Houses again appear. These were the streets of New Bryn, Cefn Road, Pleasant View, Heol-y-Twyn, Heol Llechau and Heol Ceiriog, now known as the Council Houses. After the war, in 1947, prefabs were erected, but were demolished in the 1960s and 1970s.

Thus has the village grown from rural beginnings up to today. Some things have changed since the early days, when oil lamps and scrubbed sanded floors were the norm. Unmade roads, gas street lamps and horse-drawn carts delivering goods, distempered walls and outdoor toilets were far removed from the cosy, warm palaces we have today.

Wattstown was a full and busy place during the first half of the century, but the demise of coal and the final closing of the pit brought about social changes which affected not only our village, but the whole of the Welsh valleys. With the discovery of coal and its exploitation during the years 1860-1911, the valleys witnessed a population explosion on a scale not seen before. The population of the two Rhonddas approximately 3,500 in 1860, increased to 152,000 by 1911. Wattstown became a part of that explosion as people flocked here from all over Wales and the southern English counties of Somerset, Devon and Cornwall.

With such an influx of people seeking work in an area of few houses, overcrowding became a problem, and living conditions were difficult for the early immigrants to 'Cwtch'. Finding accommodation often meant living in 'partments', and two or three families under one roof was not unusual. Eating, washing and surviving in one room created problems of health and cleanliness. The lack of pithead baths meant washing in front of the fire, in a tin bath, every day! The beds were often in use day and night; as each shift arrived home, so the other left for work, leaving behind a warm bed for the next one.

28

The wages were enough to keep the family fed, and little else. Mother was expected to 'turn collars', darn socks, wash clothes in the tin bath, by hand, and keep the house tidy, with food on the table by the time the breadwinner came home. They were the good times, when work was available. So, often, the miners' struggle for better working and living conditions was met with lock-outs, lower wages and strikes, and there were no hand-outs for anyone. People faced grim days, not enough food to feed the family, no money to buy the necessities of life. Through this, it was often the wife and mother who made such a contribution to the quality of life that, at best, was hard, drab and colourless. They knew the price of coal in hunger, anguish and loss and, in times of crisis, it was an unremitting struggle against poverty.

It was this struggle which bound together those who shared a common lot, where neighbours who had little, gave to those who had nothing. Many were encouraged to grow their own produce, so allotments and gardens were put to good use. Many kept pigs, for nothing is wasted on a pig - even half a head would make brawn.

Miss Alice Barrow, who came from Somerset to see her sister in Hillside Terrace in 1905, tells of her walk from Porth station in the rain. The roads were 'unmade', without tarmac, and with her long dress soaked, and covered up to her knees in mud, she arrived at Hillside Terrace to find that the home of her sister and husband had flagstone floors with a thin covering of sand.

The children from the first twelve houses of Pleasant View at the lower end of the street, in 1924.
They include: Annis Thomas, Megan Jones, Blodwen Thomas, Beryl Wilmore, Billy Lewis, Wyndham Jones,
Merlin Langford, Fred Trow, Sarah Williams, Gladys Thomas.

This view shows clearly the absence of motor cars in the 1930s. How clean and neat Wattstown looked then. At the bottom of the photograph can be seen the allotments and gardens below the farm road, where some members of the community kept pigs and chickens, as well as growing flowers and vegetables.

A view taken during the war years of the 1940s.

Another view taken during the 1940s. How run down the gardens have become.

View showing 'Glenside' and the shops of 'Evans the Butcher' and 'Marks,' the tin shed on the corner of Pleasant View and Cefn Road, circa 1935

*A view of Wattstown showing the Boys' Club and the rear of the Butcher's Arms.
The railway was still operating passenger trains and the goods yard when this photograph
was taken in the late 1950s.*

A view taken in 1962, when the Butcher's Arms and the Boys' Club were still in use.

Another view taken at the same time.

Her first impression of Wattstown was not a good one, but one which those who lived and worked here recognised very well. It was far removed from the often picturesque beauty of the countryside from which many of them came.

The houses themselves were reasonably well built, but decoration was simply distempered walls, usually in dark blue or green, sometimes with varnished doors. It was rare to find wallpaper, as this was expensive, while linoleum and coconut matting came much later, in the years between the wars. Carpets were for the wealthy, so sand would be spread on the floors to keep the stones clean, and swept up with the dirt. Toilets were shared by all those in the house, and usually situated outside in the back yard, while the humble china pot under the bed saw much service during the hours of darkness!

Under such conditions, the men and women of Cwtch lived and worked, and from this there emerged a community which fought to overcome its difficulties. By their own courage and endurance, they created a community spirit nourished with a rich culture of political and social awareness.

Taff Vale Railway

The Taff Vale Railway came to Eirw, just below Porth, in 1841 and eventually reached Ynyshir in March 1849. This served the collieries of Ynyshir until the line was continued up the valleys, reaching Ferndale by 1856. The Rhondda Fach incline was recognised as being difficult — a 1 in 60 gradient at Ynyshir and 1 in 55 at Tylorstown. The line continued to be used as a freight service, carrying mainly coal. Passenger services began in 1876 between Porth and Ferndale, when a halt was erected in Wattstown.

This was closed as a station on 12th July 1920, but the goods yard and depot remained in use until 7th October 1963. The passenger service ceased to operate on 15th June 1964. The older members of our community can just remember using the halt to begin their Sunday School trips to Barry Island, among them Mr Jack Lloyd, New Bryn; Mr Reg Holland, Pleasant View; and Mrs Evelyn Madden, Aberllechau Road. Even in later years, the passenger train dropped off the newspapers for Day's shop, while the goods depot continued to offer a service until 1963. One of the persons who delivered the goods from the depot was Mr Beale, of Hillside Terrace, who operated a horse and cart service.

Wattstown Goods Yard of the Taff Vale Railway, circa 1900.
The sidings and buildings were removed in 1963, when all train serv-ices to the Rhondda Fach came to an end.

The timetable of the Taff Vale Railway Company never included the Wattstown halt, except for goods, but most people who used the train remember the walk to Ynyshir station, which was the nearest 'main' platform and booking office.

Every Friday and Saturday
CHEAP WEEK-END TICKETS

WILL BE ISSUED BY ANY TRAIN TO

Porthcawl

Via Llantrisant, as under :—

Stations from which cheap tickets are issued.	Fares for to-and-fro journey.			Stations from which cheap tickets are issued.	Fares for to-and-fro journey.		
	1st Class.	2nd. Class.	3rd Class.		1st Class.	2nd. Class.	3rd Class.
	s. d.	s. d.	s. d.		s. d.	s. d.	s. d.
Treherbert ...	8 0	5 9	4 0	Merthyr. ...	9 0	6 0	4 6
Treorchy ...	7 9	5 9	4 0	Pentrebach ...	8 0	5 9	4 0
Ystrad	7 6	5 3	3 9	Troedyrhiw ...	8 0	5 6	4 0
Llwynypia ...	7 0	5 0	3 9	Merthyr Vale ...	7 6	5 0	3 9
Dinas	7 0	4 9	3 6	Quakers Yard ...	7 0	4 9	3 6
Ferndale	7 6	5 3	3 9	Aberdare ...	8 0	5 3	4 0
Porth	6 6	4 9	3 3	Aberaman ...	8 0	5 9	4 0
Hafod	6 6	4 6	3 3	Mountain Ash ...	7 6	5 3	3 9
Pontypridd ...	6 0	4 0	3 0	Penrhiwceiber ...	7 0	5 0	3 9
Treforest ...	6 0	4 0	3 0	Abercynon ...	6 6	4 9	3 3
Church Village	5 6	3 9	2 9				
Llantwit ...	5 6	3 9	2 9				

The tickets will be available on forward journey by any train having a through connection on day of issue.

Passengers booking on Fridays may return on the following Saturday or Monday, and passengers booking on Saturdays may return on the following Monday or Tuesday.

Children under Twelve years of age half-price.

The issuing of Through Tickets is subject to the Conditions and Regulations referred to in the Time Tables, Books, Bills, and Notices of the respective Companies and Proprietors on whose Railways they are available; and the holder, by accepting a Through Ticket, agrees that the respective Companies and Proprietors are not to be liable for any loss, damage, injury, delay, or detention caused or arising off their respective railways. The Contract and liability of each Company and Proprietor are limited to their or his own railways.

Photocopy of a railway timetable for 1904

FOURTEEN-DAY EXCURSION TICKETS

WILL BE ISSUED ON WEEK DAYS. TO

*Tenby, *Fishguard and Goodwick,

*CARDIGAN, *LLANDYSSIL, *NEWCASTLE EMLYN,

AND

ABERYSTWYTH,

Via **Llantrisant**, or via **Treherbert and Briton Ferry**, as under :—

FROM	Fares to and Fro, Third Class.				FROM	Fares to and Fro, Third Class.	
	* To Llandyssil.	* To New-castle Emlyn.	To *Tenby, *Fishguard and Goodwick, and *Cardigan.	To Aber-ystwyth.		To Tenby, Fishguard and Goodwick, and Cardigan.	To Aber-ystwyth.
Treorchy .... Ystrad ... Llwynypia ... Dinas ... Maerdy ... Ferndale ... Tylorstown ... Ynyshir ... Porth ... Hafod ... Pontypridd ...	12/-	13/-	13/-	13/6	Aberaman Abercynon Merthyr Vale Ynysybwl Taffs Well Treforest Cowbridge Cross Inn	12/6	12/6

First Class Tickets issued at Double the above Fares.

The tickets to Cardigan are available *via* Newcastle Emlyn on forward or return journey. Passengers using these tickets *via* Newcastle Emlyn will be required to make their own arrangements for conveyance by road between the two towns. Passengers holding backward portion of these tickets from Cardigan, wishing to commence the return journey at Goodwick or Haverfordwest, also Passengers holding backward portion of these tickets from Goodwick, wishing to return from Cardigan, Haverfordwest, or Letterston, will be allowed to do so ; but the fares do not include conveyance between these towns.

* Passengers booked to these Stations are not allowed to return on Saturdays and Mondays, from July 16th to September 10th inclusive, by the 10.55 a.m. or 1.0 p.m. trains from New Milford, but for the convenience of such passengers, a train will leave Whitland at 1.30 p.m. and Newcastle Emlyn at 12.30 p.m. on Saturdays and Monday (calling at the principal stations.)

Passengers for	Cardigan and Tenby	...	...	travel via	Whitland.
,,	,, Fishguard and Goodwick	...		,,	Clynderwen.
,,	,, Llandyssil and Newcastle Emlyn			,,	Carmarthen.
,,	,, Aberystwyth	...	...	,,	Pencader.

Children under Three years of age, Free ; Three and under Twelve, Half-price.

Photocopy of a railway timetable for 1904

Public Houses

THE BUTCHER'S ARMS

A view of the Butcher's Arms, looking across the river bridge, circa 1960.

Until 1856, farms were the only buildings in Cwtch. The Taff Vale Railway had reached Ferndale, to serve the pits that would soon spring up in the Rhondda Fach. That year, William Lewis of Brecknockshire, and his wife Mary, built the Butcher's Arms. William was a butcher by trade and a publican. They had two sons, David and Richard, who also became butchers. William Lewis died in 1865 and his widow was left to carry on running the Butcher's Arms. Her daughter, Catherine, later married William Williams, a miner. He died 10 years later, and Mary and Catherine, with their families, were left to carry on the business, which they did until 1908.

The 'Butchers' became a busy place in the 1880s with the sinking of the pit. People came looking for work and a place to stay. The first five houses of Aberllechau Road had been built in 1875, and they soon filled with families and lodgers alike. Catherine, it is said, was a businesswoman who took out life insurance policies on men who worked in the colliery. With life underground dangerous and risky as it was, she probably felt that she was on to a good thing! She also undertook the responsibility of removing the more argumentative customers, who were encouraged to cross the road to the spare ground where they could settle their own arguments. Quite a character! She had a friend who appears in the 1891 census – Elizabeth Lewis. She lived in Dinas and travelled each day by horse and cart to work in the Butchers. She became the grandmother of Ben and Lewis Davies of Pleasant View.

The next publicans to take over the Butchers were Tom and Dinah Thomas and their daughters Glenys and Iris, from Skewen.

On the night of June 22nd 1920, a disastrous fire burnt the building to the ground. Working there at the time were Nellie Uzzell and Miriam Rees, and in the haste to save some belongings, Miriam and Tom Thomas received burns.

There were no fatalities but when the Butchers was rebuilt in 1922, there was a new landlord and Tom Thomas and his family returned to Skewen.

The new landlord was Dr J. J. Hughes and his new wife, Martha. Dr Hughes was a locum working with Dr Davies of 25 Aberllechau Road. Martha had kept the Wattstown Hotel with her husband, George Hill, until his death in 1922. Dr Hughes and Martha

Tom Thomas, the licensee of the Butcher's Arms, 1908-1920

took over the Butchers and kept it until his death in 1933. He had given up his medical career to become a publican.

When he died, Martha kept it going until her stepdaughter Beryl took over. She followed her father and her stepmother in the tradition of Catherine Lewis before her. During the 1920s, when Dr Hughes was there, the 'Buffs' met in the Butchers, having moved from their room in the 'Tommy Johns'. In later years they moved back to the Tommy's.

Glenys and Iris Thomas, the daughters of Tom Thomas

41

The main entrance at the front of the building led through double doors, on the right of which was a small bar in which a group of men would meet to discuss the topics of the day — people who didn't consume much beer, but enjoyed a serious discussion about the issues that affected their lives. Miss Phyllis Owen, when home on a visit, would often help by cleaning and wiping dirty glasses while listening to them debating.

To the right of the main entrance was a single door above two steps which led to the 'Jug and Bottle', a small window and counter where women could buy beer in their own containers to take away, or sit on the bench provided and enjoy their glass. In those days, women didn't normally enter public houses, a tradition which disappeared during the war, as women became more liberated through working in factories and arsenals for the war effort.

Beryl Hughes kept the Butchers going throughout the war years and retired in 1947.

Idwal and Evelyn Roberts followed her as landlords, with their daughter, Ellen. It was during this time that the building was partly converted into flats with two upstairs and one downstairs.

In 1953, Robert Vincent Edwards, with his wife Mary and daughter Pamela, took over as the new landlord. They remained there until 1962, when Raymond and Irene Williams became the landlords, for less than two years, to be replaced in 1964 by Trevor and Muriel Lewis. Finally, William and Nancy Jones took over the job until the Butchers closed its doors in 1970. It was demolished soon after.

A list of the people who lived in the flats at the Butcher's Arms from 1949 until 1970:

Miss Sarah Jane Benjamin	Nancy M Jones
Melissa Jolley	Dorothy Saint
Kathleen Welch	Phyllis Huggins
Richard L Welch	Terence Gill
Winston Ellis	Eira Gill
Anne G Ellis	Terence Lewis Cresswell
Anastasia Jones	Norma Cresswell
George William Harvey	William J Jones
Gwenllian Harvey	Ronald James
Rosslyn Evan Leyshon	Rachel Jones
Rhianydd Leyshon	Gillian Willis
Clifford Hughes	Richard Palmer
Doreen Hughes	Kathryn Palmer
Donald Huggins	Eileen Owen

From the *Glamorgan Free Press* and *Rhondda Leader.*   24th May 1930

WATTSTOWN

Members of the Wattstown Lodge of the R.A.O.B. met at the Butcher's Arms Hotel, Wattstown on Wednesday, to hear the Reverend J Meredith Morris, B.A. (vicar of Ynyscynon) lecture. Many old Buffs recalled with what interest they gathered in the past to hear the lectures of the present lecturer's father, the late Reverend W Meredith Morris (vicar of Clydach Vale). The present lecturer dealt with the high ideals of Buffaloism, and dealt in a profoundly interesting manner with four different ages and the messages they carried to this present age. The lecture made a deep impression, and received the closest attention. Mr James Baynham, K.O.M. occupied the chair, supported by Messrs William Jones, R.O.H., H. C. Jordan, K.O.M., Tom Hughes, K.O.M., W. Brown, K.O.M., J. J. Hughes, C.P., John Pugh C.P., and others.

During the evening, excellent musical items were rendered by Messrs Ted Evans, J. J. Hughes, John Pugh, W. Brown, A. Preece, Tom Hughes, J. McIntyre; a duet by Messrs William Jones and Ted Evans and the *Buffs Song* by Mr H. C. Jordan. Mr David Jenkins played all the accompaniments. On the proposition of Mr James Baynham from the chair, supported by several brothers, hearty thanks were accorded to the Rev Meredith Morris for his effective address. A successful evening closed with the singing of *'God save the Queen'*.

Wattstown Lodge of the 'Buffs' (R.A.O.B.), 1926

THE WATTSTOWN HOTEL

The Wattstown Hotel, circa 2000

Between 1881 (the year that the National Colliery was sunk) and 1891, the population of the Rhondda rose from 55,632 to 88,351 people. Within the next 10 years, it would double the figure for 1881. This astonishing growth was due mainly to immigration, as the coal boom attracted the needy and adventurous from far afield. Housing was slowly being built to accommodate this great influx of people and, to help satisfy this need, Miners' Hotels were springing up in the valleys of South Wales.

The Wattstown Hotel was built in 1892 for that purpose. It was not a public house at first, and did not hold a licence to sell alcohol until 1904. The first landlord and subsequent licensee was Thomas John. His name will be forever linked with the pub, known ever since as 'Tommy Johns'. He remained at the Wattstown Hotel until 1907, when he moved to Ynyswen and became the landlord of the Baglan Hotel, by the Ynysfeio Colliery.

The Public Bar of the 'Tommy's' circa 2000

The next landlord of the Tommy's was George Hill, and his wife Martha, who lived on the premises until 1922, when George died. During these years, the hotel was home to the 'Buffs', who met there during the war years 1914-1918. Jimmy Wilde, world flyweight title holder from 1916 – 1923, often fought exhibition and sparring bouts in the long room of the Tommy's, sometimes against local men such as Bunny Osborne of Pleasant View.

During the 1921 strike, when the miners were in dispute with the government over wages and conditions, a force of police from Gloucester were stationed in the long room of the Tommy's as a precaution against any repeat of the riots that had occurred in Tonypandy in 1910. Food had to be prepared for policemen and residents alike, and Miss Owen, who was born there in 1914, recalls eggs being boiled, a dozen at a time, held in a pillowcase.

Her parents, George and Gladys Owen, were friends of the landlord and helped behind the bar and in the cellar. One of Miss Owen's memories is of the 'Buffs' singing *To Absent Friends*.

Mr and Mrs Hill were also assisted in the running of the hotel with a dozen housemaids, who lived on the top floor. They served the customers, cleaned the tables and the dozen brass spittoons, which had to be polished every day!

After the death of her husband, Martha Hill married Dr J. Hughes and took over the Butcher's Arms. The new landlord of the Tommy's was Thomas John Lloyd, and his wife Elizabeth, who came to Wattstown from Solva, Pembrokeshire, as many others had done before them. They had six daughters and three sons, one of whom was killed in the Great War of 1914-1918. Two of his daughters settled in Wattstown — Glenys married Jack Lloyd of New Bryn and Blodwen married John Seldon.

The Wattstown Hotel became home to the Wattstown Motorcycle Club, formed by Robert Clarke, who kept a garage opposite the pub. He organised motor cycle races in the Park, and entered many races throughout Wales, often winning against great odds. The Wattstown Quoits Team met at the Hotel in the late 1920s and 1930s, under the captaincy of Robert Williams.

In 1937, the Tommy's was taken over by William George Bainton and his wife, Catherine. Their daughter, Bessie, married Thomas Brinley Evans (Tib Evans), a teacher in Aberllechau School, and they made their home in the pub.

The next landlords to take over in 1947 were Ron and Gwyneth Lee, and their son Adrian. They kept the Tommy's for many years and made some alterations to the interior, building up the business.

In the year 2000, the Wattstown Hotel became a Listed Building, as an 'unaltered example of an early Miners' Hotel, of large and sturdy proportions'. It has served the people of Cwtch for over 100 years, and hopefully it will continue to do so for another century.

The Wattstown Quoits Team based in the Wattstown Hotel, champions of the Rhondda League in 1930-31.
Thomas John Lloyd, the licensee, is seated in the front row centre behind the Cup.
The captain of the team was Robert Williams.

The National Colliery

The National Colliery in 1887, the year of the disaster which killed 37 workmen and injured 6.

'CWTCH' COLLIERY, WATTSTOWN

Much has been written about 'Cwtch' Colliery, known as the 'National', Wattstown, regarding the terrible disasters which have occurred there. The life of the village was centred around the colliery on which most of its earliest inhabitants depended for a living.

The life and fortunes of the colliery affected the village itself — work brought wages to feed and clothe the family of the miner, but strikes, lock-outs, short-time working, lowering of wages, depression, death or injury, all took its toll upon those who worked there, far worse than on the owners themselves.

Life in the early days was never easy, often harsh and brutal, with real poverty, and yet the adversity and difficulties only seemed to forge a strong community spirit which created an environment of ambition to educate and improve the standards of life for the miner and his family.

I could never hope to cover all its history — that would be a lifetime's work in itself, so I shall keep to the known facts and hopefully, with a few photographs, help to stir your memories and remind you of a few forgotten faces, and of a companionship and neighbourliness which will never be seen again. This is not just the story of the National, it is the story of the community in which it stood for 87 years.

The pit was sunk on the site of Aberllechau Farm. The mineral rights were leased from the landowners, Crawshay Bailey, in October 1881 by Ebenezer and Henry Lewis, and Matthew Cope. They sunk No. 1 and No. 2 shafts to a depth of 454 yards.

During the next couple of years, the ownership of the colliery changed hands — first to Messrs Griffiths & Company and then, in 1884, to Messrs Watts, Watts & Company, who later, in 1887, became the 'National Steam Coal Company'.

The Company changed names, becoming the 'National Collieries Company Ltd.' and, later, the 'United National Steam Coal Company Ltd.' It became a public limited company in 1893.

Henry Lewis was the first manager of the colliery, known then as 'Cwtch'. Each new owner replaced the manager with one of their own and in 1887, at the time of the first disastrous explosion, the manager was Mr J. H. Williams and the agent Mr Edgar Watts, while his brother, Mr Hugh Watts, was the managing director of the National Steam Coal Company.

Women workers on the surface of the National Colliery in the late 19th century.

These photographs were taken from a glass magic lantern slide.

Colliers outside the Lamp Room at the National Colliery in 1887

THE 1887 DISASTER, NATIONAL COLLIERY

On Wednesday, 18th February 1887, an explosion occurred in the colliery, which resulted in 37 workmen being killed and 6 injured. This took place near the end of the day shift, at 6.40 p.m.

The report of the official inquest stated that . . . 'the operation of the colliery was conducted in a loose manner, that is, not as carefully as the case required. The cause of the explosion was the result of firing a shot without proper precautions, at the junction of Cwm Nedd and Risca headings. The report also stated that only one seam was in use at the time, it being the 'four foot', which was 'of a dry and dusty character'.

The workings of the pit were divided into five districts, namely, Harris's heading, Salvation district, Palmer's district, The Straight, and Cwm Nedd. There were two shifts, employing 200 men on days and 67-70 men on nights.

List of Those Killed

Some of those killed lived in the new streets of Hillside Terrace and Bailey Street.

Daniel Davies	aged 22	stoker
Walter Bevan	aged 30	haulier
David Owen	aged 33	farrier
Frank Belbin	aged 26	haulier
Henry Wilford	aged 32	saddler
Richard Arthur	aged 60	ostler
John Price	aged 29	hitcher
Samuel Richards	aged 27	haulier
Albert Shewry	aged 24	engineman
Daniel Jones	aged 52	collier
William David Williams	aged 14	collier boy
Richard Pritchard	aged 42	contractor
William Roberts	aged 22	haulier
William Guy	aged 18	labourer
Griffith Griffiths	aged 51	overman
Thomas Tovey	aged 28	cogman
Morgan Davies	aged 40	roadman
David Edwards	aged 24	fireman
Richard Bryant	aged 24	labourer
Morris Davies	aged 28	ripper
Henry Davies	aged 32	collier
John Charles	aged 22	collier
John Evans	aged 34	ripper
John Curley	aged 36	collier
Charles Williams	aged 25	collier
Watkin Jones	aged 23	collier

Richard Powell	aged 37	collier
Morgan Gibbon	aged 26	collier
John Lewis	aged 32	collier
Phillip Jeffries	aged 28	collier
Thomas Morgan	aged 38	collier
William Llewellyn	aged 31	haulier
Oliver Clements	aged 23	haulier
Thomas Jones	aged 23	haulier
Edward Goodwin	aged 25	haulier
John Jones	aged 36	ripper
Thomas Tudor	aged 38	collier

The miners of South Wales during that time lived in an environment of danger and dependency. Coal promised work, which brought in wages, yet work in which death and injury were never far away. After the first explosion in Cwtch, the miners had no redress, nor were they protected by any legislation regarding safety in the mines. These matters were left to the 'wisdom' of the mine owners.

The National was considered to be a modern mine in the years leading up to the 20th century, yet we know that carelessness would lead to more deaths before many years had elapsed. Kier Hardie, the Scottish M.P. for Merthyr, stated in 1910 . . . 'a dead pony is £20 lost; a dead miner costs nothing except heartache for those left behind.' Following the first disaster, the owners Watts, Watts & Co. installed electric lighting, making this the first colliery in South Wales to be completely illuminated by electricity.

In 1894, the upcast shaft was deepened by another 101 yards, to make available all the steam coal seams of the middle and lower coal measures. At this time, there were 1118 men employed in the pit. In 1891, the census showed that William Meredith, his wife, and daughter, lived in 69 Hillside Terrace. He had come to the Rhondda some time before this from Llanelli. He became the manager of the National in 1898, whilst James Miles from Risca lived at *Glenside* as the commercial agent, responsible directly to the mine owners as their representative in all matters of business concerning the mine. This position of agent was above that of the manager, and one of influence in the community which depended so much on the pit.

In 1898, the miners themselves, without a united force behind them, sought to change the agreement on which their wages were set. This had existed since 1875, known as the 'sliding scale', where wages depended on the selling price of coal. The outcome was a six months strike, which ended in favour of the mine owners. This led directly to the formation of the South Wales Miners Federation, with a membership of 30,750 men in 1899. The next 10 years were crucial in the miners' fight for safety and better conditions of work and pay. Between 1900 and 1910, over 500 men would be killed in the South Wales coalfield alone.

The Colliery, pictured on the day of the disaster.

THE SECOND DISASTER, NATIONAL COLLIERY, 1905

Chapel Street on the day of the disaster, when thousands of people gathered at the scene.

On Tuesday, 11th July 1905, at 11.45 a.m., another disastrous explosion occurred which resulted in the death of 119 men and boys. This was caused by gelignite being used to clear a barrier of coal in the cross heading from the sinking pit to the upcast pit.

There had been an accumulation of gas in this area, which exploded causing the death of 119 of those working in No. 2 pit. Gelignite could legally be used in the sinking of a shaft, but was prohibited in the mine, where gas would accumulate.

Mr William Meredith, who lived at the time at *Glenside*, was in complete charge of the colliery as manager, and had only minutes before the explosion been raised from the workings.

When the explosion occurred, he immediately descended the pit, but became one of the victims, killed by the choking effect of the afterdamp. Miraculously, the explosion had no effect on No.1 pit, where a much larger workforce of 930 men and boys were employed.

Haulage engine underground at the colliery. Note the electric motor driving the engine through gears, circa 1910.

We can only imagine the devastating effect this had upon the people of Wattstown and the mining community of the Rhondda. The news of the disaster spread quickly through the valleys. People came from all surrounding areas to find news of relatives and loved ones.

The roads were packed with thousands of people from Ynyshir, to Tylorstown, and within the village of Wattstown the school was empty, as wives and mothers, with their children, waited with dread to hear if one of 'theirs' was among those killed.

There were tragic scenes of grief as each body was identified by relatives, for some had lost one, two, or three members of their family — fathers, brothers, husbands and sons. A great sense of sadness and grief hung over the village as each day passed.

The first funerals took place on Friday, 15th July, followed by the majority of bodies being interred on Saturday. More followed on Sunday. Thousands and thousands lined the route to Trealaw (Llethrddu) Cemetery as the slow moving cortege passed by. They stood, in silent respect, to the singing of Welsh hymns - sung with a sadness that fitted the sorrowful occasion.

The last body was recovered on Sunday, 20th July, and work continued to repair the damage done to the pit and to resume normal working as soon as possible.

The inquest took place in Porth on July 31st, where the undermanager, Mr. Evan Williams, was the first witness called.

The report of the inquest gave the opinion that shot-firing should be absolutely prohibited except between shifts, and that only shot-firers should be in the pit at the time. The regulations regarding the issue and use of explosives were not adhered to, and again this 'loose attitude' had been the cause of another disaster. Lessons from 1887 had not been learned.

A report by the company commercial agent, Mr Walter T. Griffiths, stated that the explosion had left 44 widows, 110 fatherless children and, of those killed, 56 were under the age of 20 and 33 under the age of 15.

The whole grim story underlines the dangers and risks involved in coal mining. The National was a model of up-to-date equipment and produced, then, about 1500 tons per day of the very best steam coal available. Yet, in spite of this, the dangers always existed. Life itself in the mining communities was difficult enough, with no luxuries, and drab conditions.

Life revolved around the mine and the hours it imposed upon its workforce to earn a living for families, often with upward of 10 or 12 children to feed and clothe. Many who came to the valleys came from rural areas, where life was no better and often poorer. Coal meant work and work offered money and a chance to improve one's lot.

List of Those Killed

John Reeves	aged 19	62 Hillside Terrace
J. W. Dando	aged 27	
William Eastman	aged 45	29 Bailey Street
Thomas Lillycrop	aged 25	18 School Street
William Meredith	aged 55	Manager, Glenside
William Jones	aged 60	29 Aberllechau Road
Elias Roberts	aged 25	4 Danygraig Terrace
James Baines	aged 55	
Isaac Davies	aged 29	14 Dolycoed Terrace
Richard Morgan	aged 18	35 Aberllechau Road
Arthur Kemp	aged 43	72 Hillside Terrace
John Morgan	aged 59	
Thomas Edwards	aged 23	
David G. Davies	aged 23	2 Lower Bailey
W. J. Basset	aged 14	29 Hillside Terrace
W. H. Goldsworthy	aged 20	23 Hillside Terrace
George Chidgey	aged 18	
J. M. Williams	aged 14	11 Bailey Street
Thomas Davies	aged 38	1 Hillside Terrace
Thomas Flower	aged 41	
Thomas King	aged 47	36 Bailey Street
James Gibbon	aged 48	42 Margaret Street
O. Pritchard	aged 38	
Idris Williams	aged 21	15 Aberllechau Road
John Probert	aged 20	
Edward Morgan	aged 16	
William Richards	aged 14	
Gwilym Edmunds	aged 19	
Thomas Gibbon	aged 15	42 Margaret Street
John Gibbon	aged 25	42 Margaret Street
D. J. Rees	aged 15	19 School Street
David Rees	aged 38	19 School Street
Sam Bird	aged 16	New Houses (Pleasant View)
James Healing	aged 14	32 Bailey Street
C. Davies	aged 18	1 Hillside Terrace
E. J. Sampson	aged 17	42 Hillside Terrace
John Howells	aged 42	
Thomas Howells	aged 15	

Isaac Jones	aged 17	
William Hudd	aged 16	44 Hillside Terrace
J. E. Davies	aged 18	
Flurence Mahoney	aged 17	19 Lower Bailey Street
Sef Richards	aged 46	
W. J. Evans	aged 18	
Evan John	aged 18	2 Chapel Street
R. Hallett	aged 38	
William Hallett	aged 17	
D. G. Davies	aged 15	19 School Street
D. Johnson	aged 64	51 Hillside Terrace
B. Walters	aged 37	Graig Road
Robert Cross	aged 38	
John Jones	aged 38	
John Tingle	aged 14	8 Upper Gynor Place
J. R. Walters	aged 15	
Sam Smith	aged 14	6 Hillside Terrace
W. J. John	aged 23	
Thomas Perryman	aged 19	
Thomas J. Prosser	aged 16	17 Lower Bailey Street
Fred Fletcher	aged 25	
E. Mansel Beard	aged 14	34 Hillside Terrace
Sam Mason	aged 34	35 Bailey Street
G. Perryman	aged 38	
William Perryman	aged 14	
Thomas Williams	aged 15	20 Lower Bailey Street
William Daniel	aged 40	
C. H. Davies	aged 15	
C. E. Perry	aged 19	Hillside Terrace
Alfred Uzzell	aged 40	13 New Houses (Pleasant View)
John Uzzell	aged 15	13 New Houses (Pleasant View)
George Evans	aged 26	63 New Houses
David Phillips	aged 26	
John Rees	aged 37	21 South Street
D. J. Rees	aged 15	21 South Street
R. Yell	aged 20	
A. Billett	aged 22	
David Davies	aged 37	
D. T. Morris	aged 15	

The funeral procession on Saturday, 16th July 1905, after the terrible disaster which killed 119 men and boys.

The hearse at the head of the funeral procession.

W. T. Morley	aged 27	
T. H. Smith	aged 17	
D. Williams	aged 26	15 Aberllechau Road
W. Morgan	aged 15	54 Hillside Terrace
Robert Billett	aged 34	
David Davies	aged 32	
Thomas Jones	aged 15	45 Hillside Terrace
John Davies	aged 26	3 New Houses
David Johnson	aged 16	51 Hillside Terrace
David Powell	aged 32	
John Turberville	aged 14	6 Pleasant View
Thomas Davies	aged 40	50 Hillside Terrace
W. Albert Williams	aged 13	14 School Street
Ben Lewis	aged 16	
Albert Marshall	aged 33	
W. H. Lloyd	aged 16	1 Hillside Terrace
Alfred King	aged 22	36 Bailey Street
W. M. Thomas	aged 17	New Houses
Richard Williams	aged 43	11 Hillside Terrace
Edwin Williams	aged 16	11 Hillside Terrace
John Clancy	aged 38	
C. S. Clancy	aged 17	
John Rees	aged 50	
John Rees	aged 17	
Thomas Jones	aged 51	
F. Wiltshire	aged 14	4 Bailey Street
J. Williams	aged 44	
W. H. Evans	aged 17	
Enoch Davies	aged 21	38 Edmund Street
Thomas Owen	aged 33	
William Morgan	aged 17	35 Aberllechau Road
John Morgan	aged 25	28 Hillside Terrace
M. R. Evans	aged 25	
C. E. Perry	aged 39	
J. H. Davies	aged 14	
Sam Hughes	aged 21	
F. Woodham	aged 33	
J. Evans	aged 29	4 Danygraig Terrace
D. S. Powell	aged 15	7 Chapel Street
David Davies	aged 47	

DIFFICULT TIMES

The decade of 1900-1910 was a difficult time for the South Wales coalfield. 70% of Welsh coal production was exported. The price of coal from the United States of America, France and Germany became more competitive.

This seriously affected the demand for coal from South Wales and caused the mine owners to look closely at cutting costs in order to maintain profits. Wages accounted for 60% of the costs and so the miners were expected to bear that loss with lower wages.

In 1909, Parliament passed the '8 Hour' Act, which was intended to protect the miner against long working hours, stating; 'The miner could not spend more than 8 hours underground at work, in any 24 hour period'. This seriously lowered the earning power of the miner and, coupled with rising inflation and less demand for coal, undermined the living standards of the miner's family, which were already difficult.

These problems were aggravated by the mine owners demanding a new agreement, saying that production had fallen due to the 8 Hour Act, and this led to another struggle between the miners and the owners. This dispute lasted six months, finally resulting in riots at Tonypandy by the miners of the Cambrian Colliery Company.

This did not directly affect the National, except that the ensuing agreement led to the introduction of afternoon shifts, whilst wages were still based on 1875 coal prices.

1910 saw a stronger and more militant South Wales Miners Federation emerge as a result of the tensions and battles, together with the terrible loss of life that had been a pattern of life in the South Wales Valleys for so long.

1912 saw yet another strike in the National which lasted 5 months, and soup kitchens were set up in the Workmen's Institute.

1913 was a time of stability. As war approached, so did the demand for steam coal for the Navy and this year saw the peak in coal production in South Wales, with a total of 57,000,000 tons.

The manager of the National at this time was Mr John Kane, and the agent Mr Ivor Llewelyn. During the war years of 1914 - 1918, there was full employment as the demand for coal continued. A dispute in 1915 had led to better wages and, in spite of the war effort, problems still existed.

At the end of the war, John Kane became the agent, based at *Glenside*. In 1921, he became the Secretary of the company and in January of that year he warned of approaching unemployment and short working times to come. This was the start of a general depression in the coal industry, with a fall in demand for coal as exports fell. At home, the Royal Navy and Merchant Navy switched to oil-burning ships. This seriously affected the National and ended in a 4 months lock-out as production stopped completely in the South Wales coalfield.

A report ordered by the government suggested that the coal mines be controlled by the state. The government, however, had other ideas and returned them to the original owners. The miners were at the mercy of these owners and without any other support.

The miners refused to return under the old terms and were simply locked out. When they did eventually return to work after four months, conditions were unchanged, while wage rates were actually lower! No wonder the miners felt so strongly about their situation.

A report in the *Western Mail*, 14th April 1921, reads:

"From early morning, the miners of Maerdy, Tylorstown, Ferndale and surrounding districts gathered into three huge processions, headed by its own band. After 9 a.m., they set off for the National Colliery, where safety men were still at work. They eventually numbered 5000 men, who wore red rosettes and red ribbons in their hats.

They assembled outside the colliery offices, and while negotiations took place, the great crowd sang *The Red Flag*. Eventually, the management agreed to the immediate withdrawal of 36 officials. The demonstrators then marched back up the valley, singing and playing *Land of My Fathers* and *Men of Harlech*."

1921 saw the opening of Wattstown Memorial Park, built at a cost of £10,000 by the National Steam Coal Company, and opened by Sir Shadforth Watts, the president of the company. This became a welcome amenity in the community.

There was a temporary boost to production in 1923 -24, which collapsed in 1925, and thus began a prolonged depression which lasted through to the end of the 1930s.

Conditions at the National hadn't changed very much. Deaths and injuries still occurred. Mr Reg Holland of Pleasant View was completely buried under a roof fall in September 1924. There were no medical facilities, no baths available and no transport for those needing hospital treatment. He survived the fall and was taken to the surface in a coal dram.

Another miner carried Reg on his back as far as Hillside Terrace, where he was fortunate to be seen by Noel Davies, who worked for Thomas & Evans of Porth. He gave Reg a lift on the back of his truck to Pleasant View — it seems that the truck had to reverse up the hill as it was too steep to climb it in forward gear.

Not every story ended happily, however, and a report from the *South Wales News* of March 1926 said: "Sympathy is expressed at the death of Mr. Steve Atkins, aged 18, of Pleasant View, who worked at the National Colliery as a collier's helper for four years. The little family of nine children, having lost their parents, were under supervision of their grandmother and the responsibility for their support fell heavily on Steve. It seems a particularly hard stroke of fate that he should have had to lay down his charge at this stage."

1926 was the year of the General Strike. The miners were out for 7 months and the result was even more poverty and dire distress for the families of Wattstown. The strike affected everyone, and soup kitchens were set up at Calfaria Chapel.

The intention was to help those in real need and there were many such people. The soup kitchens were run by volunteers who were often in much need themselves. The food was contributed by companies like Thomas & Evans and by groups such as Fry's, the cocoa and chocolate company, who were Quakers. The shopkeepers, too, were aware of the need and often gave credit to their customers, readily agreeing to wait for payment until employment restarted.

It was this year which saw the National change hands. David Davies (Lord Llandinam) of the Ocean Colliery Company bought a controlling interest in United National Coal Company and so began another chapter in the story of Cwtch.

Mr John Kane, who had been an influence in the community of Wattstown, retired from his position as General Manager of the group of companies in July 1927. At a presentation in his honour, Mr J. S. Vincent, the manager of the National, paid tribute to his long service and loyalty to the company and to the community he had served as Councillor and Justice of the Peace.

The end of the prolonged strike in 1926 saw the closure of many collieries, due to poor or non-maintenance during the months of stoppage.

This was the beginning of the decline of the mining industry in South Wales, as the demand for coal at home and abroad fell rapidly. This caused other pits to close during the following decade.

The Ocean Coal Company, however, began a modernisation programme in its existing pits and in 1928 the National was offered free pit head baths by the administration of the Miners' Welfare Fund, under the following conditions:

1.   The company would supply the ground and clear it.
2.   It was to be managed by eight trustees, including four workmen.
3.   It was to be maintained by sufficient numbers of colliery workmen.

The baths were to be something very different in the life of the miner, and many were reluctant to even think of using them! The thought of going home clean, today, seems very sensible and we don't have to use tin baths in front of the fire! It has been said that some believed that washing one's back made you weak! In spite of these initial objections, the baths were built by late 1929 and became one of the first pits in the Rhondda to have such modern facilities.

1930 saw another slump in the coal industry and the National was shut down again for several weeks. This was the situation that continued with monotonous regularity.

In 1930, the Local Mines Act introduced minimum prices and restrictions in output. None of these helped the miner and the 1930s saw many strikes, lock-outs and sit-ins at the National. In 1933, the country was still feeling the effect of the 1926 slump and by January, 2.75 million people were unemployed.

Dangers still existed in mining and in March 1932, William Davies of School Street died of injuries received at work, leaving behind a widow and 10 children. In 1935, underground miners at the National were offered hard hats! It seems strange in this day and age of 'Safety First', that men should be charged 1/6 (7½ new pence) for a miner's helmet.

During these difficult times, the management of the National changed frequently. In 1926, when the National became part of the Ocean Coal Company, Mr J. S. Vincent was the manager. He was followed by Mr H. E. Marshall, a Risca man, who remained until 1929, when Mr Evan Evans (Silent Evans) returned to the colliery as manager, with Mr Rhys Dodd as under-manager.

In 1934, Mr Levi Phillips lived at *Glenside*, as agent, and Mr W. Payne Bundy was under-manager. Many of our older citizens will remember these names, and many more.

By the late 1930s, war was imminent and the demand for coal rose and employment remained steady. Many of the miners entered the forces. In 1937, 1100 men were employed at the National, but by the end of the war when the coal industry was nationalised, the figure had fallen to 749.

Nationalisation brought with it new hopes for the miners and their families. Now, they looked forward to having twelve days annual holiday instead of six and even the possibility of a pension scheme and a five-day working week with a £5 minimum wage.

With nationalisation, the colliery became part of the National Coal Board's South Western Division, No. 3 Area, No. 1 Group and employed at that time 190 men on the surface and 560 underground, with the South Pit working the six-foot seam and the North Pit working the Red Vein, six foot and No. 2 seams. By 1954, the manpower was 789, working the Bute, Yard and Upper Seven Feet seams, producing that year 184,000 tons.

1960 saw an even greater production of 203,162 tons, with a manpower of 585 men. Towards the end of its life, the N.U.M. Lodge at the National was concerned enough to complain of the run-down state of the colliery, which resulted in poor working conditions.

The National was finally closed on 22nd October, 1968, the end of an era for Wattstown. The closure of the mine was a mixed blessing. Jobs were lost, which seriously affected the miners, of course. Businesses closed, realising the loss of trade would cause them to fail. It was a way of life many would find difficult to adjust to, although adjust they did, and found the new conditions in factories etc. far more amenable.

The wives and mothers, on the other hand, had different thoughts: no more uncertainty, no longer waiting and worrying if their husbands would come home safely, no more risking life, limbs and lungs. One, Bronwen Williams, said in the *Rhondda Leader* report, she had twelve sons and all went to the pit. "Don't go today", she would ask them, "I hated the pits, but there was nothing else".

The sinking of the pit was the birth of our village, the very reason for its existence. It is over 30 years since its demise - what will our future hold? More changes, of that we can be certain. With its ending, a whole way of life passed into history. The harsh, difficult days of the early years forged a close-knit community. People shared with their neighbours the dangers and despairs, finding an outlet in the social and cultural life of the chapels and churches, the Institute, the pubs and the Boys' Club.

Every organisation became a part of the life that was Wattstown before the war of 1939. The National stood in the centre of this community, the place of toil and comradeship.

The very conditions of life caused many to leave the area in the 1920s and 30s for better wages and prospects - the very same promises that the colliery itself had made to the immigrants of 1880 from the rural areas of Wales and England. Those days will never return for us - we have moved on, into a more affluent century, but the close ties of those early days, forged by a companionship of danger and dirt, will long be remembered with a certain amount of sadness and longing.

Edgar Richardson, Will Stuckey and Charlie Norris on the surface in August 1953.

View of Wattstown, overlooking the wagon sheds and Lower Bailey Street.
The wagon sheds were built by the Ocean Coal Company when they took control of the National in 1926. As they expanded their coal operations, the need arose for more new wagons, and repairs to the existing stock. The sheds continued to be used under the ownership of the N.C.B. but were closed in February 1957.

Hauliers on the surface at the National.

The National Colliery Ambulance Team in 1939. They entered in the National Competitions, and won on three consecutive occasions. Included in the picture are Hugh Jones, Levi Phillips, Evan Evans and Alf Evans (Ynyshir)

Levi Phillips, with Hugh Jones, holding the Ivor Llewellyn Shield, having won it for the third time, and Evan Evans

Group of surface workers at the National, August 1953

Back row (left to right): Harold Rug, Hughie Jones, Evan Morris, Cliff -, Evan Edwards, Sam Rose, Eddie Thomas, Jack Davies.
Front row (sitting): Reg Brown, Tommy Griffiths, Len Davies, Dai Walters, Norton Day, Randy Stroud, Tommy Stevens

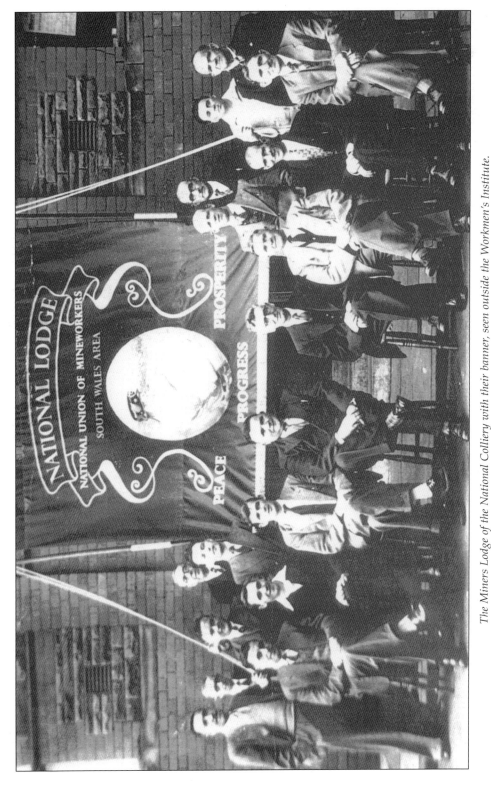

The Miners Lodge of the National Colliery with their banner, seen outside the Workmen's Institute.
Back row (left to right): Dai Thomas (Sarge), Len Jones, Jack Lloyd, Tommy Kenealy, Alf King, Ned Jones (Hangman), Alby Uzzell, Bunny Johnson.
Front row: W. J. Thomas, Eddie Peel, Idris Griffiths, Billy Woods, J. Jones, Mog Thomas, Ivor Rowlands, Alwyn Evans.

Ladies visiting the National.
Standing on the left is Hugh Barrow, and one of the men on the right is Wythan Hughes.

Visitors to the colliery, including Maureen Locke, Cath Smith and Trevor Thomas

Mr Jack Jones being presented with his retirement gift by Mr Bundy, the manager of the National

Visitors about to go down the National Pit in 1968, just before it finally closed.
Included in the picture are: Mildred Watkins, Neil Watkins, Lily Daniels, Edna Davies,
Lynfa Jones, Glyn Davies, John Jenkins

View of the National from the railway bridge, circa 1962

Looking at the colliery from the Arcade, circa 1962

73

Another view taken in 1962

The last day of the colliery

The last tram of coal from the National Colliery, October 10th, 1968.
Included in the picture are:
Jack Lloyd, Ivor Jones, Tommy Edwards, Cyril Banky, Tal Wigley, Tommy 'Res'.
The verse was written by Amos Griffiths.

The 'Arcade' bridge over the railway cutting behind Aberllechau Road

76

Filling in the cutting

The colliery site after the pit had been dismantled and cleared

Chapels and Churches

As the village grew with the opening of the colliery, so did the needs of the community around it. In 1891, 70% of the people of Wattstown were Welsh speaking; the majority of those who came to the 'Klondike' that was Rhondda, and Wattstown in particular, came from other parts of Wales, where the Welsh language was still strong. This is the oldest language in Europe and can be traced back to Roman times. In this strong Welsh-speaking environment, it was natural that the chapels which sprang up at that time were Welsh. The Crawshay Bailey estates were in the ownership of his daughters, Mrs Canning and Mrs Curre, who were keen to see Christian worship introduced into the community and freely allowed land to be leased for this purpose. The ground would be leased and the building erected in a short period of time.

The chapels were often a satellite of the mother church which existed elsewhere, and the new buildings catered for the needs of the population explosion. As the industrialisation of the valleys continued at a fast pace, the need for building skills increased and those who built the chapels and churches were called upon to erect work places, public houses and other buildings such as colliery 'sheds', which is why so many buildings of that time have a distinct resemblance to chapels.

The employers recognised the link between sobriety, industriousness and non-conformity, and encouraged the thrifty, hard-working chapelgoer, for association with a chapel could mean the opportunity for advancement at work and even being employed at all! The Taff Vale Railway, which served the Rhondda Fach, stated in its rule book of 1856 for employees that, 'It is urgently requested of every person on Sundays and Holy Days that he attend a place of worship as it will be a means of promotion when vacancies occur'.

This later became an even harsher fact of life when the colliery manager and his officials became deacons in the chapel, for those who advanced themselves in this way became an influence in their community. Not only did they have a position of authority at their work, but also a place in the 'set fawr'. The chapel was often the centre of the community, the place for 'Magic Lantern' shows, cantatas, concerts, Sunday School teas and, of course, the annual trip to the seaside. Now these have been overtaken by television, bingo halls, and the private motor car which makes it possible to travel anywhere at any time.

The life of the chapels in Wattstown was relatively short-lived, but they continue with Bethel, in School Street, and, until 1998, St Thomas's on Hillside Terrace. The Royal Commission on places of worship, in 1910, stated there were 150 Non-Conformist chapels in the Rhondda alone, where the trinity of chapel, workplace and the rugby pitch became a feature of life.

ST THOMAS'S CHURCH

When St Anne's Church in Ynyshir was built in 1886, it was the outcome of a need, expressed by the influx of people into the parish. This led to a similar situation in Wattstown, where the population explosion was just as great, at a time when Welsh chapels were already in existence.

The earliest meeting of the parishioners in Wattstown took place in the 'Board' school, so named because it was run by the Llanwonno School Board. On July 20th, 1896, a site was leased from the Crawshay Bailey estate, for a period of 99 years, at an annual ground rent of £4. An 'iron' building was erected and opened on September 18th, 1896 at a cost of £800, including all works and surrounds etc. It was originally intended to seat 250 people; whether it actually did, I know not.

The cost of the building was found by the members themselves, except for a gift of £100 from the Bishop of Llandaff's Fund, which was intended to encourage such undertakings as forming new churches. St Thomas's and St Anne's were in the joint parish of Llwynypia and Llanwynno and shared the incumbents, based at Ynyshir.

The first vicar of St Thomas's, in 1896, was the Rev Samuel Jones, who had been curate at Llangynwyd from 1883 to 1893 and became vicar of St Anne's and St Thomas's from 1893 to 1910.

He was followed by such names as Rev Llewelyn Davies of Lampeter, curate, Rev Pierce Price B.A. in 1919 and Rev Thomas Williams, vicar, in 1925. It was during his period of office that, in 1931, the interior of the church building was refurbished.

These renovations were completed by 1932 and in February of that year, the church was re-dedicated with a service conducted by Rev L. T. Hopkins, Rev J. H. Fisher, curate, and Rev Thomas Williams, vicar.

The work, which had taken 5 months to complete, included a new sanctuary, chancel and vestry. The furnishings, and other gifts were donated as follows:-

Seating of Chancel and Altar Cloth	*Rev T. & Mrs Williams, Ynyshir*
Oak Litany Desk	*Rev J. H. Fisher*
Oak Credence Table	*Rev Wynne Roache, chaplain H.M. Forces, Portsmouth*
Linen Cloth for Table	*Mrs Roache, Ynyshir*
Carpet for Sanctuary	*Mr & Mrs H. Davies, Ynyshir*
Processional Cross	*Mr & Mrs E. J. Reeves, Wattstown*
Pair of Oak Candlesticks	*Miss Fisher, Cardiff*
Lino for Chancel	*Mrs Bailey, Wattstown*
Lino for Nave	*Messrs Clapp and Ford*
New Altar Frontal	*subscribed for by members of Ynyshir and Wattstown churches*

St Thomas's Church, from a painting by Ken Baker

Arthur Ford, builder, and other men of the church, namely Idris Wiltshire, Walter Lovering, John Jones and Jack Bailey, carried out the renovations. This greatly increased the size of the building and gave the interior a sense of space, which it previously lacked.

It was originally intended to be only a temporary structure, but it remained so for over 100 years, as it was never rebuilt. A coal fire, situated in a room beneath the main building, heated the interior of the church. This fire was able to provide heat, which rose through a grid in the church floor. On cold mornings, this grid was easily found, as the parishioners eagerly gathered around it to keep warm. It was a cheap form of heating, with free coal from the National. With the nationalisation of the colliery in 1947, the supply of free coal ended, and the church was converted to electric heaters mounted on the walls.

In the 1980s, other work became necessary, and with the Reverend Earl Hastie's encouragement, the parishioners raised the money. They built a new kitchen and toilet, fitted a suspended ceiling, which helped to cut the cost of heating, and new lights and gas convector heaters were installed. These changes certainly made for a more comfortable church. St Thomas's and St Anne's were both served by the same vicar and his curate. It was usually the curates that served St Thomas's for most services, and you will find a list of their names at the end of this chapter.

As in every church, each priest brings his own talents and abilities, and each will always be remembered for his strengths and weaknesses. However, the church continues in the life of its parishioners, and over the past 100 years many will be remembered for their loyalty and commitment to the cause of St Thomas's. Here we are able to recall some of those names.

The first person to be christened in the new church was Joseph Warren Morgan, who was born on January 6th, 1887, and for many years tended the church garden.

Bert Jordan, who became the Superintendent of the Sunday School, and a lay preacher; Mrs Ford, church organist; Mrs Nicholls, cleaner, caretaker, sacristan and general worker.

Mrs Davey, who played the organ three times a Sunday without fail, and Joe Hutchings, sidesman.

Fred Wiltshire, who became the first person from Wattstown to be a warden of St Thomas's. He held this office for seven years. Mrs Freda Wiltshire, cleaner, caretaker, Sunday School teacher, youth club leader and sacristan, and Glyn Jones, lay reader and active member in later years.

I have included the names of just a few that are still remembered, but many others have given of their time and efforts over the 103 years of the church's life. The influence of these clergy and lay workers will always be a part of the history of St Thomas's, Wattstown.

Sadly, the church building was closed for worship in 1998 and finally demolished in 1999.

Easter Vestry

The Easter Vestry meeting in connection with St Anne's Ynyshir, and St Thomas's Wattstown was held at St Anne's Church Hall on Wednesday evening and was a successful event. There was a fair attendance. The vicar, in an address, stated that the church membership had increased, and a good year's work in many directions accomplished.

Financially, there had been a reduction as compared with previous years. This was due, no doubt, to the unfortunate state of the collieries locally. The Vicar's Warden, Mr A. E. Ford, read the balance sheet, which had been audited by Messrs J. Reed and E. Harry Davies.

The report was accepted. Mr Ford was reappointed Vicar's Warden and Mr E. Harry Davies was elected People's Warden. The following sidesmen were elected. St Anne's (People's): Messrs H. J. Davies, D. Jarman, W. Daunter, T. Leyshon, S. Parr, and James Pugh. Vicar's: Messrs J. Vaughan, C. Maxfield, W. David Williams, E. Reakes, J. Barrow and J. Williams.

St Thomas's (People's): Messrs J. Hutchings, A. Clapp, G. Perrow. Vicar's: Messrs H. Griffin, T. Preece and W. King. Members of the Parochial Church Council elected were: Mrs T. Williams (Vicarage), Mrs E. Roach, Mrs (Dr) D. H. Davies, Mrs Yeoman, Mrs Richards, Mrs T. Jones, Mrs Robins, Messrs J. Reed, T. Jones and T Leyshon. Mrs Evans (Glenside, Wattstown), Mrs Clapp, Mrs Ford, Mrs Davey, Messrs G. Perrow and T. Preece.

The efficient Secretary of the council, Mr Herbert C. Jordan, was re-elected.

BETHEL FREE MISSION

Bethel Free Mission, circa 1955

The revival of 1904/05 brought together members of the community who were challenged to find a place where English-speaking people could worship. Many families and individuals were arriving from English counties, seeking work in the colliery. Whereas the village was mainly Welsh speaking, this was changing, and the challenge was taken up by Thomas Bowen, Oliver Draisey and Samuel Cardin.

They met in Mr Bowen's house, 67 Hillside Terrace and Mr Cardin, who owned a grocer's shop (later to become Terry Stores), offered the use of a room in his house as a place of worship. This became too small and the warehouse under the shop was put at their disposal.

Thus, the small congregation grew as the population increased, and a Sunday School was formed, which soon required a larger building. They established a building fund and worked to raise money. The sewing classes made items to sell, while the young people who met each week performed cantatas and concerts.

In 1915, they heard of an old army hut for sale. This was a building of wood and corrugated iron which could be assembled on site. Mr Bowen, Mrs Tom Evans and Mrs Alice Hicks went to view it and purchased it for £5. The Crawshay Bailey estate were helpful in finding a plot at the end of School Street where Bethel still stands today.

The deacons of Bethel photographed in their Jubilee year of 1955 – D. Rowlands, A. Viner, W. Mainwaring, F. Vaughan, J. Clements, C. Starr

The interior of Bethel, circa 1955

The manager of the National Colliery, Mr John Kane of Glenside, and the colliery owners, the Watts brothers, allowed the building to be brought to the National by rail, and helpers hauled it up in sections to the new site.

The original 15 members worked hard to make the building usable and, with the help of many members of the community, built foundations, laid drains, and water, gas and toilets were installed.

All was completed at a cost of £58, which came from the building fund and from donations. The church building was opened by the Rev James Rees of Tonypandy and it was called Bethel Free Mission.

The membership continued to increase and the Church prospered. The ministry was in the hands of people like Thomas Bowen and others, while the preaching was carried out by local lay preachers; Richard Johns was appointed Pastor, a position he held for many years.

In those early days, the church was strengthened by a Sunday School, teenage groups and new members. Among those were the following:

Eileen Isaacs, Jennie Phillips, Beatrice Bowen, Dolly Phillips, Ruby Taylor, Elsie Barrow, Doris Evans, Ivy Norris, Myra Norris, Vanno Llewelyn, Olive Gully, Harold Evans, Louise Phillips, Dolly Phillips, Edna Morgan, Fred Morgan, Harold Gully, Bert Russell, Albert Uzzell, Ernie Dyer, Ernie Hicks, Jim Macintyre, Jed Minty, Tom Phillips, Tom Phelps, Edwin Potter, Tom Thompson, George Thompson, Hugh Barrow, Ronald Norris.

First Account of Church, 1905

	INCOME					EXPENDITURE			
			£	s.	d.		£	s.	d.
Feb.	5			6	6	Planks for Chapel		11	0
	12			6	6	Oil		4	0
	19			3	4	Oil and jack		2	2
	26			3	7	Lamp Glasses			11
				19	11	1 Bible for Table		2	0
						Oil for lamps		1	5
March	5			5	6	Planks		11	0
	12			5	7	Mrs. Morgan		1	0
	19			6	1	Oil for lamps		1	1½
	26			5	4	Mortar, 6d. ; Size, 9d.		1	3
			2	2	5	Nails, 6d.; Whiting, 1/-		1	6
						Turpentine			6
April	2			7	2	New Lamp		3	6
	9			4	9	2 months rent	1	4	0
	16			4	6½	Planks		5	6
	23			4	3	Oil			11½
	30			15	0	Gas Fittings & Glass		1	9
			3	18	1½	Whiting		1	0
						1 months rent		12	0
May	7			4	2	I doz. Testaments		4	0
	14			4	7½				
	21			5	6				
	28			4	11				
Total A/c			£4	17	4	Total Expenses	£4	10	7

Bethel as it is today, circa 2001.
This was built in 1975 after the original building was destroyed by fire in 1973.

One of the first Sunday School scholars to marry was Miss Jenny Phillips to Mr Hugh Barrow after the first world war. The Sisterhood began meeting in the Workmen's Institute during the 1914 -1918 War, where Mrs John Kane of Calfaria played the organ. They moved to Bethel Church eventually and continued with Mrs Alice Hicks as president for 30 years.

The church continued to grow and was very active, so that in 1925 the building was extended at a cost of £100 and a new organ costing £27 was obtained. It was reopened and consecrated by the Rev R. B. Jones of Porth, Mrs W. R. Jones and Miss Thomas of Ynyshir. In 1933, a new roof was fitted to replace the one that had been added to. In 1945, the freehold was purchased.

During the 1920's, Mr Watkin Mainwaring became conductor, organist and treasurer of the church until his death in 1960. In later years, others took up the responsibilities of the church, including Frank Vaughan, Charlie Starr, Jack Clements, Selwyn and Gwenda Gough, Rene Bosley, Vi Liddell, and others.

Sadly, in 1973, the original church building was burnt to the ground. The members met for a while in the school dining hall, which itself had once been a chapel (Nebo). A new prefabricated building was erected on the original site and opened after two years, in September 1975.

This is the present building of Bethel, which celebrated the first 95 years of its existence in the millennium year of 2000. Its membership may have decreased, but its presence and influence in the community is still strong. Long may it continue.

This section on the Welsh Chapels was written by Eben Phillips, the last secretary of Calfaria. He now holds this office in Ainon, Ynyshir. Eben is a descendant of one of the first families to settle in Wattstown in the 1880s, being the great grandson of David Lewis, who had a butcher's shop in Aberllechau Road.

CALFARIA

Calfaria Welsh Baptist Chapel, 1894-1969

Most of the original inhabitants of Wattstown were Welsh speaking and among them were a number who spoke no English. They came from other parts of Glamorganshire, Monmouthshire and rural Wales, bringing with them their Welsh culture and traditions. At first, they attended the Welsh chapels already in existence in Ynyshir - Ainon (Baptist), Saron (Congregational) and Tabernacle (Methodist) and, later, Moriah. The Welsh chapels in Wattstown were offshoots of these churches in Ynyshir.

The first Baptist in Cwtch was Lewis Evans of Tirgwaidd Farm, a member of Salem, Porth and later Hermon, Pontygwaith, where he was responsible for starting a new cause in the 1860s.

The Men's Class in Calfaria Wattstown, circa 1910.
Most of these names have not been identified, but included are the following:
Morris Jenkins, Hillside Terrace (first left, back row), David W Thomas, Heol y Twyn (5th from left, back row), David Evans (3rd from left, middle row, postmaster and father to Maggie the Post), Rev Christmas Jones (5th from left, middle row. He lived at 9 Chapel St), Vaughan Evans, Bryn Terrace (3rd from left, front row and father of Phoebe Evans)

The Baptist witness in the new community of Wattstown dates from 1886 and they were the first to organise prayer meetings and a Sunday School. They met in the home of Mr Isaac Hughes, Hillside Terrace, for that purpose.

As the Baptists grew in number, they had to move to larger premises – first to a stable loft, then to a room at the pithead and finally to the Long Room in the Wattstown Hotel. It was not unusual for embryonic churches to use such premises. At that time, the Wattstown Hotel was not licensed to sell alcohol. It was there, in February 1894, that 80 men and women formed themselves into a Welsh Baptist Church, which they called Calfaria.

With seating for 700, Calfaria Chapel was built in the autumn of that year at a cost of £2,200 – a mighty sum in those days. The site chosen was the bedrock of the river, to reduce the risk of subsidence.

By the end of 1894, an additional thirty had been baptised, increasing the membership to 110, with 190 in the Sunday School. The first secretary was Mr David Evans who, at that time, lived at 21 Danygraig Terrace.

Ladies serving in the soup kitchens outside Calfaria during the 1926 Miners' Strike

Mr Evans was a poet, and later moved to Aberllechau Road to keep the Post Office. He was the father of Miss Maggie Evans the Post. The first minister was the Rev Edmund O. Parry, who came from Ainon, Ynyshir to establish the new church. He remained in Wattstown for four years, returning to his native Montgomeryshire in 1898. His youngest daughter, Miss Ceridwen Davies, who was born in Wattstown, has now died at the age of 105 in Llanfyllin.

There followed two short ministries by the Rev T. M. Williams (1902-04) from Wrexham and the Rev O. J. Owen (1905-08). Shortly after Mr Owen's arrival, an explosion occurred at the National Colliery, killing 119. A number of these men were members of Calfaria, including the colliery manager, Mr W. Meredith. His daughter married John Kane, of Glenside, and she was the organist at Calfaria until the family moved to Cardiff in the 1920s.

Mr Owen was a very powerful preacher and had a sound influence on the life of the community. If he met any of the male members of his flock slightly the worse for wear on a Saturday night, he would remind them of the Sabbath the following day and they made sure they were in chapel on Sunday evening. Mr. Owen left Wattstown in 1908 to become the minister of one of the largest Welsh Baptist chapels in Wales - Caersalem Newydd, Abertawe.

In 1909, the Rev E. Christmas Jones left a church in Merionethshire to become the minister of Calfaria and remained for nine happy years. Mr Jones was very popular, loved by his people and held in high regard by everyone in the village. His ready smile dispersed many a dark cloud and during his time in Wattstown he was referred to as the 'kind Samaritan'.

The church flourished - in 1910 he baptised 35 and the membership reached 168. He left to take charge of Salem Welsh Baptist Chapel, Cardiff, but he continued to visit Wattstown to take services at Calfaria for many years afterwards. At his farewell meeting, held just a few weeks prior to the Armistice of 1918, Mr Jones was presented with a purse of gold, Mrs Jones received a bible and fountain pen and bibles were also given to the three children.

Local talent provided the musical items at this meeting, with contributions from the Wattstown Male Voice Party, conducted by Mr Dan James.

Up until the end of the First World War, it was the custom for many to attend the Sunday evening service even though they were not chapel members. They were called 'Gwrandawyr', i.e. Listeners/Adherents, and included many children, not always attentive, who used to sit in the gallery. The punishment for misbehaviour was to sit downstairs with their parents. The presence of these 'Listeners' helped swell the evening attendance in Calfaria to between 250 and 300. However, during the 1920s, they virtually disappeared from the congregation.

It was nearly three years before Calfaria had its next minister, Rev Price Evans, a native of North Wales. He remained for twelve years, moving to Carmarthenshire in 1933. The task facing Mr Evans when he arrived was not an easy one.

As a consequence of World War I, there was a certain disillusionment with organised religion, especially among men. Counter-attractions continued to undermine the role of the chapel, which at one time had been the main focus of community life. Many Welsh-speaking parents failed to pass on the language to their children. The inflow of Welsh speakers virtually ceased after 1921. Indeed, during the 1890s, many monoglot English speakers came to live in Wattstown. Their arrival severely diluted the Welsh character of the village and it became one of the most anglicised areas in the Rhondda, and the Welsh chapels suffered accordingly. The year 1926 witnessed the seven months Miners' Strike, followed by the Depression, when many left to seek work across the border in England.

These factors led to a decline in Calfaria's membership — from 120 in 1919 to 75 in 1933. Attendances also fell because many *gwrandawyr* (listeners) simply drifted away. The same story was repeated in Carmel and Nebo.

Nevertheless, Mr. Evans, a kindly man, did his best for the chapel and the community. He stood for Christ outside the church as well as within. During the long, hot summer of the Miners' Strike in 1926, he organised soup kitchens in the vestry and he got the men to decorate the interior of Calfaria.

He always maintained that it was a privilege to serve as a minister in the Rhondda. His departure was a great loss to the village, and many came to pay their respects at his farewell meeting, held on 29th May, 1933, when he was presented with a gold watch, and Mrs Evans with a silver teaset. The three children received hymn books. Later, his son, Herbert, entered the Welsh Baptist ministry.

For most of Mr Evans' ministry, the church secretary was Mr James Rosser, who possessed a magnificent tenor voice which helped him in his role as *'codwr canu'* i.e. leader of the singing in the chapel. He was an official at the National Colliery and lived at 3 Victoria Terrace. For a while, his daughter, Miss May Rosser, taught at Aberllechau School.

For the next eleven years, Calfaria was without a minister and the membership fell to 39 by the early 1940s. However, the usual chapel activities continued. The Sunday School flourished. Children of families in the church came regularly to the Sunday morning services, when they recited their verses and, for their efforts, were recipients of books at Christmas time.

Secular cantatas such as *Sleeping Beauty* were held in the chapel, when a stage was erected in the pulpit area. These events were very popular and were a welcome source of funds for the chapel in its efforts to reduce the onerous church debt.

On a more regular basis, magic lantern sessions were held in the vestry under the auspices of the Rechabites, who taught the virtues of total abstinence.

For a time during the Depression, Calfaria was used as a centre for the distribution of Christmas toys donated by voluntary bodies from outside the Rhondda. There was much poverty in those days and the local children were grateful to receive these gifts.

Every Mabon's Day (the first Monday in May), Calfaria children attended the annual *Gymanfa Ganu* (hymn singing festival) held in Salem, Porth, which would be full to capacity on such occasions. It was quite a thrill to go down to Porth, unaccompanied by parents, and sit in the gallery of that huge chapel. After a sumptuous tea in Salem vestry, there was the opportunity to window gaze in Hannah Street. The only money the children had was for the chapel collection, but sometimes the temptations of Woolworth and Longstaff's Penny Bazaar proved too much, and the evening collection would be short by several ha'pennies as a result.

An important occasion in the church calendar was the Sunday School Anniversary, an event preceded by many weeks' learning 'off by heart' recitations and choruses - there were no bits of paper in hand in those days!

Perhaps the most eagerly awaited event in the year was the annual Sunday School outing to Barry Island. It was always Barry, never Porthcawl. Beforehand, the weather on St Swithin's Day was carefully observed and, on the appointed day, children and parents walked to Ynyshir station. The approaching steam engine would frighten some of the children, who would be reluctant to board the 'monster', but the thought of missing a day out at the seaside soon overcame their fears.

These outings were discontinued during World War II, but they resumed shortly afterwards. However, they were never the same again. Buses were no substitute for the excitement of travelling through the tunnels of the old Barry line.

In 1936, an eisteddfod, organised by Miss Jane Jones (Gorwel) and Mrs Levi Phillips (Glenside), was held in Calfaria. Mrs Phillips was a very active worker in the chapel during the 1930s. She was instrumental in getting a central heating system installed. She obtained donations from far and wide, including a contribution from David Lloyd George who, of course, was a Baptist himself. Mrs Phillips arranged a number of social events in the village, including garden parties at Glenside and a sports gala on the field next to the Boys' Club, opposite Calfaria.

Some of the deacons who sat in the *set fawr* (big seat) during the 1930s and 1940s include John Evans (Bryn Terrace), George Jenkins (Chapel Street), John Powell (Bank Villa) and his brother Herbert Powell (Tylorstown), Tom Wilmore (Pleasant View), John Phillips the Post (Pontygwaith), Morris Jenkins, David John Davies, and Stanley Evans (Hillside), William Evans (Bailey Street) and John Jenkins (Tirgwaidd).

The church secretary for about 20 years until the mid-1950s was Mr D. W. Thomas (Heol-y-Twyn), a very able lay preacher. He obtained the necessary qualifications to enter college to train for the ministry, but he was unable to take advantage of this opportunity.

1944 was a significant year in the history of the church. The debt was finally cleared after 50 years and Calfaria began a joint pastorate with Hermon, Pontygwaith. The new minister was the Reverend Brinley Reynolds, a native of Treorchy. Mrs Reynolds worked very hard with the young people and Sunday School before leaving in 1947, when Mr Reynolds took charge of two chapels in Llandudno.

During the ministry of the Rev Brinley Reynolds, the membership increased from 39 to 48, but after he left, there was a continuous decline to 35 (Sunday School, 34) in 1951, to 20 (Sunday School, 28) in 1957 and to 12 (Sunday School, 25) by the late 1960s.

The outlook was bleak, with only about half a dozen attending services. The prosperous days of the church were but a faint memory. The maintenance of such a large building was too much for the few that remained and in 1969 they had no choice but to close Calfaria. Of the remnant, the majority transferred their membership to Ainon, Ynyshir where only two remain. Thus ended a vital chapter in the history of Wattstown. For a while, the chapel was used as a builder's warehouse until it was converted to flats by the Cameron brothers in the mid-1980s.

Sir Edgar Rees Jones. M.A., K.B.E. (1918)

Born in Cwmamman 1878.

He was called to the Bar, Grays Inn in 1912. He became the Liberal M.P. for Merthyr Tydfil 1910-1915, and Merthyr Division 1918-1922. During the war years 1915-1918, he worked for the government in the Ministry of Munitions. He lectured in English Literature, and was a writer and orator, the son of Rev M. H. Jones of 'Gorwel', Pleasant View. He died in 1962

A prominent family in Calfaria was the Jones Gorwel family. The Rev M. H. Jones had been a minister in Pembrokeshire and the Rhondda Fawr. In 1891, the family was living in Aberllechau Road, where they kept the Post Office.

One of his sons, Sir Edgar Jones M.A., was Liberal M.P. for Merthyr Tydfil from 1910 to 1918.

He played a prominent role in the religious and cultural life of the Rhondda. Sir Edgar was a member of Calfaria and an accredited lay preacher within the Welsh Baptist denomination. He was in great demand as a chairman for chapel concerts and oratorios.

Four of his sisters remained in Wattstown and became headmistresses of local schools, the youngest, Gladys, being head of Aberllechau Infants. After retirement, they moved to Porthcawl in 1956.

THE OCEAN AND NATIONAL MAGAZINE

May 29th, 1933

CALFARIA, WATTSTOWN: A large gathering came together on Monday afternoon, May 29th, to pay tribute to the Rev Pryce Evans on his departure to Cwmdu, near Llandilo, to take over new churches, after twelve and a half years at Calfaria Baptist Church, Wattstown.

In the afternoon, a farewell tea was held, attended by a great number of friends and ministers of the district. In the evening, a large audience attended the presentation to Mr and Mrs Evans and their three children. The meeting was presided over by the Rev John Edwards, Salem, Porth.

The following ministers all paid tribute to Mr Evans:

Revs: R. Griffiths, Moriah, Pentre
   J. Williams, Salem, Ferndale
   S. Thomas, Hermon, Pontygwaith
   D. Thomas, Soar, Penygraig
   W. O. Jenkins, Calfaria, Clydach Vale
   C. Davies, Nebo, Ystrad
   G. Davies, Saron, Ynyshir

The following laymen also spoke:

Messrs: E. J. Reeves, Wattstown
    G. Young, Tylorstown
    W. Thomas, Hermon, Pontygwaith
    A. Thomas, Ainon, Ynyshir
    D. Thomas, Calfaria
    E. Thomas, Bethel
    D. Morgan, Nebo
    E. Roberts, Carmel
    Mr Daniel Evans, Free Church Council

Mrs J. Lewis, Ferndale, of the Zenana Women's Guild, spoke with much feeling of the fine qualities of Mrs Pryce Evans.

Rev Pryce Evans was the recipient of a gold watch, formally presented by the senior deacon of Calfaria, Mr John Evans, milk vendor.

Mrs Evans was presented with a silver tea service by Mrs Ceinwen Thomas, and each of the three children received a hymn book from Mrs Irene Edwards.

Mr and Mrs Evans feelingly, and appropriately, thanked all for their good wishes.

The Rev John Edwards, as usual, kept the meeting in good humour.

The departure of Mr Evans will be keenly felt by all who knew him intimately, as he was always so ready to give a helping hand to all and sundry who sought his aid.

The Rev Pryce Evans was a very popular and respected man during his time spent in Wattstown, and many will remember him during the tea parties in Calfaria, when he would carry two jugs, and in his strong North Wales accent ask, 'Tea or Cocoa?'. This name has remained and will always bring to mind this kind man.

The Rev Pryce Evans, minister of Calfaria, 1921-1933

The wedding reception held in Calfaria school room, after the marriage of
Mr Lionel Bosley and Miss Irene Rowlands, on August 11th, 1956

The other half of the family

THE OCEAN AND NATIONAL MAGAZINE

March 1939

'THE KING AND THE COBBLER': Sparkling performances of the children's operetta entitled *The King and the Cobbler* were given at Calfaria Baptist Chapel, Wattstown, by the Calfaria Band of Hope Choir, on Wednesday and Thursday, March 10th and 11th.

Conducted by Mr Brynmor Mainwaring, Wattstown, the choir sang delightfully, and it was evident that they had been carefully trained. All the characters were attractively dressed and the scenery was excellent. The dances were efficiently executed and everything went off with a swing.

It is worthy of mention that the conductor is a young Wattstown man making his first appearance in this capacity. He is better known as the accompanist of the Pontygwaith Harmonic Choral Society.

The accompanist was Mrs Irene Edwards, Wattstown, and the dances were under the direction of Mr Oswald Morgan, Pontygwaith. The presidents were Miss J. M. Jones, Gorwel, Wattstown, and Mr J. Rosser Harris, headmaster of Pontygwaith Schools (Pencerdd Penrhys), on Wednesday and Thursday, respectively.

The principal characters were:

The King	-	Mr J. Richards, Ferndale
Premier	-	Mr Oswald Morgan, Pontygwaith
Physician	-	Mr Evan Jones, Tylorstown
Jester	-	Mr Gwilym Morgan, Wattstown
Cobbler	-	Mr Evan Jones, Ferndale
Page	-	Master Allen Smith, Wattstown
Flower Girl	-	Miss Betty Lewis, Wattstown
School Maid	-	Miss Gwyneth Hughes, Wattstown
Lady Golfer	-	Miss Sue Morris, Tylorstown
Cook	-	Mrs Joan Williams, Ynyshir

There were also choruses of cricketers, footballers, glee maidens, and teachers.

CARMEL

Carmel Welsh Independent Chapel 1897-1939 as it stands today, It originally consisted of a smaller vestry at the rear of the building, but was extended to its present size in 1906.

Saron, Ynyshir, was instrumental in starting a Welsh Congregational Chapel in Wattstown. It gave generously towards its establishment and is rightly regarded as the mother church of Carmel. In 1895, Saron re-started a Sunday School in the village and, soon afterwards, prayer meetings and the occasional preaching service were organised. The venue for these activities was the colliery band room.

Two years later, Saron built a vestry. The building cost of this and the upper room came to £632. The opening service took place on 16th October, 1897. Thereafter, all meetings were held in the new premises, apart from the monthly communion services, when the members went down to Saron. By 1903, the fellowship of 45 felt strong enough to form themselves into a separate church, and this they did on 16th December, 1903.

A leading figure in the church, then, was Dewi Heulwen, of Hillside. At that time, the chapel debt was £415. Saron made a gift of £315, leaving Carmel members to finance the remainder.

A group of boys from Carmel Sunday School with their teacher, Mrs Daniels, of Hillside Terrace. The banner belongs to the Christian Endeavour Movement in the church.
Back row (left to right): Jimmy Ball, —?, Owen Morris, Marshall Morris, Eben Davies.
Front row: Emlyn Rosser, Jack Collins, Mrs Daniels, Idris Griffiths, Jimmy Tandy.

The chapel was built in 1906. Although not as large as Calfaria, the chapel and vestry provided accommodation for about 400. The huge debt was a constant worry for the members and was doubtless one of the main reasons why Carmel had to close just over thirty years later. The Rev James Williams was the minister from 1905 to 1918, when he moved to the Afan Valley and later to Breconshire. He returned to the Rhondda during his retirement, living in Treorchy. For many years, the secretary was D. Watcyn Jones, of 16 Bailey Street. He was followed by Trevor Davies, of 26 Brewery Street, Pontygwaith. The last person to hold this office was Sam Jones, of 44 Pleasant View.

As in Calfaria, the usual chapel activities took place. Carmel also had a Drama Society for a while. Both chapels held 'Big Meetings' *(Cyrddau Mawr)* twice a year, when famous preachers would conduct services on Saturday night, Sunday and Monday. In years gone by, these meetings always attracted large congregations. They continued in Calfaria until the 1960s, but by then the numbers attending had fallen dramatically. In 1914, Carmel had 124 members, with 85 in the Sunday School. After the First World War, the membership decline was continuous, falling to 114 in 1922 and 81 in 1930. In an attempt to attract new members, English replaced Welsh as the language of worship in the mid-1930s, but this failed to stem the decline.

In 1938/9, although there were 59 on the Sunday School roll, only 23 members remained. This fact, and the onerous debt, forced the chapel to close. The building was sold and Carmel became a factory.

(During the Second World War, the Wattstown Home Guard met in Carmel, using it as their headquarters. Among the Home Guards were Joe Morgan, Robert Ely, Joe Hicks, Evan Davies, Tommy Rees, Tommy Ward, and Jack Bailey.)

THE OCEAN AND NATIONAL MAGAZINE

CARMEL DRAMATIC SOCIETY

The production of the drama *'Change'* (J. O. Francis), at the Workmen's Institute, Wattstown, on January 10th and 11th, was voted an outstanding success, and two repeat performances had to be given, on January 25th and 27th.

The producers, Messrs Sam Jones (fireman) and Edward Roberts (collier) are to be complimented upon their coaching of a combination hitherto entirely new to the drama, and a booking for a further four performances (in aid of other churches) must be encouraging.

Mr Dan Jones, J.P., Porth, and Mr Levi Phillips, Glenside, acted as chairmen.

The cast were as follows:

John Price	-	Mr Bob Evans
Gwen	-	Madame Daniel
John Henry	-	Mr Leslie Harris
Lewis	-	Mr Syd Owen
Gwilym	-	Mr Haydn Evans
Sam Thatcher	-	Mr William Evans
Lizzie Ann	-	Miss Elsie Williams
Isaac Pugh	-	Mr John M. Jones
Jenny	-	Miss Bernice Daniel
Twm Powell	-	Mr Cecil Evans
Dai Matthews	-	Mr Keston Daniel

Mr J. M. Knott was the stage manager, and Mr Jack Jones looked after the secretarial work.

Incidental music was played by Miss Ada Dickson.

NEBO

Nebo, Welsh Calvinistic Methodist, 1904 -1934.
For years it was used as the school dining hall, but now is a play school for young children.

The last and the smallest of the Welsh chapels to be established in Wattstown, with seating for 200, was Nebo Methodist, Victoria Terrace, in 1904. The Reverend T. J. Williams became minister in 1908 and stayed for a few years. About the same time, one of the members, David Rees, left to train for the ministry at Trefecca College, in Breconshire.

During its brief existence of about 30 years, Nebo never had a large membership, as the following figures reveal:

Membership	Members' children	Sunday School Roll	Teachers	Average Attendance
1912/69 *incl. 5 deacons.*	41	83	16	64
1924/46 *incl. 3 deacons*	44	70	13	56
1930/32 *incl. 3 deacons*	28	77	8	55

Nebo Sunday School Class, circa 1910.
Included in the photograph are Greta and Gwladys Jones of 'The Boot Exchange', Pontygwaith.
Greta stands centre back row; Gwladys is seated second from left.

Nebo closed in the early 1930s and the chapel became a centre for the unemployed, where men were taught the rudiments of various trades. Later, it was used by the school meals service.

Connected with the chapels of Wattstown, like chapels elsewhere, were men and women who, though perhaps not in possession of gifts of great talent, learning or wealth, were nevertheless guided by constant principles and gave of their best. Like the Workmen's Institute in Victoria Terrace, the chapels were examples of communal solidarity. They helped maintain a worthy tradition representing all that was best in our communal experience. Wattstown is a poorer place, spiritually and culturally, as a result of their demise.

Schools

Aberllechau Infants, Standard 1, circa 1895

Aberllechau Infants, Standard 4, circa 1897

ABERLLECHAU SCHOOL

The school was opened in 1887, by the Llanwynno School Board, which was responsible for education in the parish of Llanwynno. It was known as the Board School, and consisted of the upper part of the present building. On the 7th of February, 1889, the Infants and the Mixed departments were separated, and head teachers appointed for each section. The headmistress of the Infants' School was Miss Elizabeth Gronnow, who had been a teacher there since the opening of the school.

During the early years, the school closed for Mabon Day. This was a holiday, won for the miners by William Abraham (Mabon), local M.P. and leader of the Miners' Federation. This meant that most of the children stayed at home to enjoy the day with their families. Truancy was a real problem, and, under the Education Act of 1870, parents were held responsible for their children's attendance. Because of this, school attendance officers called regularly at the school for a list of the most frequent absentees. The parents were liable to prosecution and a fine of 5 shillings by the school board.

The early days were often hard and difficult times for families and in 1891 it is recorded that 8 paupers were paid to attend school for 1/- (5p) fee, while children from Margaret Street and Furnace Road were kept away from school because of smallpox in their homes.

The insanitary conditions of the times, and overcrowding of the school, often meant that sickness reached epidemic proportions and caused the school to be closed by the M.O.H. as a precautionary measure. Diphtheria, cholera, and smallpox appeared, but as conditions gradually improved, measles, mumps, and scarletina became more common ailments.

Discipline was sometimes a problem, even 100 years ago. One week in September 1892, fifteen panes of glass were broken in the school, while in 1894, David William Davies, of 10 New Terrace (Bryn Terrace), who persisted in throwing dirt and stones at school windows, was told to go away. A written complaint was sent to his father. The following day, his mother came to inform the Head that she was unable to control him.

On January 2nd, 1895, the school became the responsibility of the Ystradyfodwg School Board, as the whole of the Rhondda Fach became part of the new Authority. Up until that time, the river was the boundary between Llanwynno parish on the east side, and Ystradyfodwg on the west.

The number of children attending the school was increasing rapidly, and by 1896 there were 155 in the infants department alone. The teachers complained regularly of the big classes (60-70) in premises that were far too small.

The staff consisted of Miss E. Gronnow, the headmistress, two pupil teachers, and one assistant. Apart from the headmistress, these were older girls who were invited to pursue the profession on a four-year apprenticeship.

Many would withdraw after experiencing the difficulties of large classes and problems of discipline. It could not have been easy for the pupil teachers, who were little more than children themselves. Boys were also invited to become pupil teachers, but many parents refused to sign their indentures, preferring them to find work in the colliery, which paid better wages.

July 1905 saw the tragic death of 119 men and boys in the National Colliery. As a result, the school was empty of children, and was closed for two weeks as families mourned the death of so many loved ones. Hardly a family was untouched by the disaster.

In 1906, Miss Gronnow retired, and Miss Elizabeth Phillips took her place as the new headmistress of the infants school. One of the happier occasions, which closed the school, was a Royal Visit or Royal Family event. In 1909, King Edward VII visited the Rhondda and the Bailey Estates trustees gave all the schoolchildren a party to commemorate the occasion.

By now, well over 200 children were in the infants department, and conditions were becoming very difficult for the staff of six. The mixed school averaged 264 pupils, with a staff of eight. This time, another influx of people into Wattstown meant more houses being built in Victoria Terrace and Pleasant View, and the overcrowded school was enlarged to accommodate the extra children. The schoolroom of Nebo had been used as temporary classrooms since 1902 and now, with an average of 264 mixed pupils and 152 infants, it was time for a more permanent building to accommodate them.

The Rhondda Education Authority eventually agreed to build the much-needed new school and on 23rd April, 1909, Mr Alban Richards, of Ton Pentre, was successful in tendering for the job. The lower school was completed by October 1910 and accommodated 262 infants, while the earlier building was to accommodate 334 mixed pupils. It seems incredible today that there were over 600 children in Aberllechau School at any time.

The headmaster of the mixed school was Mr Daniel Phillips, while Miss Elizabeth Phillips remained as head of the infants section.

No records exist for the mixed school until April 1913. The infants and the mixed departments were always affected by the same circumstances, the only difference being the staff and the academic results. These are listed at the end of the chapter. Circumstances were never good in the community, and a prolonged strike at the National Colliery meant that the children had to be fed from soup kitchens set up in 1912 in the Workmen's Institute. The teachers volunteered to assist in this, as families found it difficult to make ends meet. Now that there were 212 infants listed on the register, and with three teachers sick with influenza, the difficulties increased. As war approached, many pupils saw their fathers register for the forces, and in 1914 another Royal Visit to the Rhondda gave them another day off. Teachers whose fiancés were home on leave were given time to see them before they returned to France. In 1916, Mr David Moore left the staff for military service and returned a year later to continue teaching.

Aberllechau Mixed Standard 1, circa 1913
Mr Daniel Phillips, the headmaster, stands left of the picture and a very young David Moore to the right.

Occasionally, teachers were given Monday off to assist in the war effort. The Annual Singing Festival held in Saron, Ynyshir was a big occasion, as the schoolchildren played a large part in the proceedings, and were given another day off. Fathers and husbands returned to France as the war raged on into 1918. An outbreak of measles and whooping cough early in the year resulted in many absentees.

As the war effort continued, a tank arrived in Porth, which caused much excitement and the absence of many pupils again! By June, an epidemic of influenza began in the Rhondda which eventually caused the death of over 300 people and closed the school for 8 weeks.

The end of hostilities in November was celebrated with three days holiday. Unfortunately, the celebrations were overshadowed by the epidemic, which caused the death of Mrs Humphreys, a teacher in the mixed school, in December. The death of a pupil or member of staff was always a sad occasion, and it was customary, as a mark of respect, for the whole school and staff to line the roads of Wattstown as the funeral procession passed by.

After the end of the Great War, there was a sense of optimism in the country as the people looked forward to happier times. However, in March 1919, the teachers were in dispute with the Education Authority over pay, and went on strike for the month. Another Royal Visit in June, when the Prince of Wales visited the Rhondda, set the pattern for the year with another day free from lessons.

The bakers went on strike and children were kept home because of the bread shortage. The Sunday Schools of Wattstown took their annual trip to Barry Island in June and there were many absentees the following day! It seems that so many went on these trips that it wasn't worthwhile opening the school for the few that were left!

The story continues in July, with a peace celebration for the children, a demonstration with the miners, and more Sunday School trips to Barry, which meant another day off. Finally, in October, the caretakers went on a one-day strike and no school fires meant that the children were sent home.

The 1920s began in a similar fashion, with outbreaks of whooping cough, scarlet fever and diphtheria, while the attendance officers regularly came to the school to list the absentees.

The Butcher's Arms burnt to the ground on June 22nd, 1920, and many children stayed up late to watch the fire, resulting in a poor attendance in the morning assembly! A couple of charabanc outings, and a half-day for the Wattstown Carnival and Sports Day, all added to the school year.

It was usual for the children to be tested on their knowledge of the scriptures by learning one of the psalms or verses from the Bible. The Rev M. H. Jones, of Gorwel, Pleasant View, originally did this and in later years Mrs Jones, his wife, or Mrs Alice Hicks of Hillside Terrace. The children's health was becoming an important part of school routine, too, with regular visits by Dr Gilder and Nurse Jones, while Miss Davies, P.T. Drill Instructress, visited the school to give classes drill in the schoolyard.

The school was inspected annually by H.M. school inspectors. Their report was usually concerned that the same problems existed, year after year. Notably the outside toilets, the small school yard for so many children, and the steps, which were dangerous in winter, especially for the young ones.

Generally, though, the report was good, and took into account the overcrowded conditions that the staff and pupils had to contend with. It was always appreciative of the standard of teaching and the fact that Aberllechau was a happy school.

In February 1921, the miners of Britain began a national strike, which lasted for four months. The schoolchildren were fed two meals a day at the school canteen in Nebo. This was done on a voluntary basis with the assistance of the teachers. As the strike continued through the Whitsun holidays, any teacher serving at that time was given time off in lieu at a later date.

The food was donated by voluntary subscriptions, and cost the ratepayers nothing. Even after the strike ended in July, some children still came to school without breakfast. The teachers fed those children at the school - the costs paid for by a Distress Fund.

Things gradually improved as the miners went back to work, and the year ended with an outbreak of mumps. 1922 began as the previous year had ended, with an epidemic of influenza with half the pupils and staff absent.

The Royal Wedding of Princess Mary to Viscount Lascelles in February was a day off to celebrate, and the official opening of the Wattstown Memorial Park by Sir Shadforth Watts, in April, gave the children a half-day to attend the ceremony. Mrs Elizabeth Phillips retired in May 1922 after 16 years as head of the infants school. Miss Elizabeth Fenwick succeeded her.

112

Royal Weddings were always occasions for the schoolchildren to enjoy, and the wedding of the Duke of York to the Lady Bowes-Lyon in April 1923 was a popular one, celebrated with another day away from school.

The death in August of Miss Olwen Williams, a nursery teaching assistant, however, was a sad occasion, as she had only been at the school for twelve months. It is interesting to note that in the school logbook from which this record is taken, some years appear not to have much of interest to report. I believe that it is probably due to a number of factors:

1. The records depended upon the person who filled out the logbook, usually the head teacher or the clerk. Thus, some wrote more than others, while some kept strictly to school business.

2. The school life was very routine, in any case, and usually only affected by sickness or the weather.

3. As health conditions improved, so did the problems associated with them decrease.

4. It is also a fact that during the 1920s and 1930s many families moved away from the area, because the depression in the coal industry encouraged people to seek employment elsewhere.

1924 seems to have followed the usual routine. Diphtheria caused seven infants to be taken into the Isolation Hospital, while two children were prosecuted for persistent absence. This was rare, as the Authorities were reluctant to go that far.

The first recorded trip for the school took place in September 1924, when 31 scholars and teachers visited the British Empire Exhibition at Wembley. It must have been a thrill for those who were fortunate enough to go. Not only was it a new experience, but it was a forerunner of the school trips which later became a regular feature of the school year.

The logbook records that the school was closed the following day to give the pupils and staff a rest after the long journey! Very little is recorded during the next two years, except that 1926 was the year of the General Strike, which lasted only nine days nationally, but was continued by the miners until December 17th. Volunteers from the staff fed the children at the school.

The Royal National Eisteddfod came to Treorchy in July 1927 and the school had a holiday to celebrate. Ice, snow and cold weather closed the school in December. Mr Ivor R. Jenkins became the new headmaster of the mixed school on 3rd April, 1928. This was the year that Mr D. Moore's wife died.

Now school trips began on a regular basis. In October, 102 scholars and five teachers visited Stratford-upon-Avon, and later that same month, 86 children and four teachers journeyed to Bristol Zoo. 1929 began with the chickenpox! And in July, 32 scholars visited London Zoo, accompanied by Miss Elsie Jones and Mr T. B. Evans. Another group of 25 were taken to Bristol Zoo a week later.

Aberllechau School, Standard 2a Mixed, 1928.

Back row (left to right): Idris Griffiths, Norman Blake, Delroy Simmonds, Peter O'Neill, David Pickford, John Evans, Jim Ball, ?, Cyril Green.
3rd row:: Norah Jones, Gwen Harris, Sylvia Williams, Hetty Williams, Dorothy Bateman, Beryl Johnson, Bessie Gowen, Nancy Long, ?, Sylvia Willis, Dorothy Taylor.
2nd row: Iris Davies, Marie Hicks, Morfydd Hughes, Megan Hudd, Sheila Sweet, Mona Lloyd, Morfydd Bowen, ?, Francis Lye, ?, ?, Iris Williams.
Front row: Delroy Parry, Jack Collins, George Carter, ?, Emlyn Rosser, ?, Paddy Kennealy.
Teacher, Miss Minnie Shibko.

Aberllechau School, Class 3, Infants, 1928.
The class includes; Jack O`Neill, Danny Condon, Glyn Ball, George Gooding, Tommy Richards, Tommy Stroud,
John Griffiths, Fred Wiltshire, Gwilym Rosser, Reg Morris, John Evans, Desmond Phelps, Betty Clarke, Betty Lewis.

Aberllechau Mixed School, Class 3a, 1928
Headmaster, Mr Ivor Jenkins and teacher, Miss Elsie Jones. One of the persons recognizable in the photograph is
Valmai Morris, who is seated on the first left of the second row. She worked as a bus conductress on the Rhondda buses
during the war years.
Two others are also included, Bernice Daniels and Olwen Rees.

Aberllechau Mixed School, Class 6a, 1928.
Headmaster, Mr. Ivor Jenkins and teacher, Miss Florence Rowlands. The only other person recognizable, is Edwin Peel,
fifth from the left in the back row, who was a member of the National Lodge of Miners Union, and became Underground
Dispute Agent, a position he held for many years.

Aberllechau School. Std 7a and Std 8 Mixed, 1928.
Back row (left to right): . - , - , Cliff Williams, Glyn Rowlands. -, -, -, Emlyn Jenkins, -, Phil Dixon.
2nd row: Griffiths, Bessy Townsend, Emily Williams, Gladys Jenkins, Ada Ball, Gwen Williams, Elunid Pickford,
Violet Williams, Catherine Thomas, Joanna Atkins, Robert Walsh,
3rd row: Derwen Crewe, Phyllis Maddern, Enid Davies, Enid Bird, Annis Thomas, Mair Morris, Muriel Horler,
Nancy Jarman, Phyllis Owen, Barbara Evans, Mabel Stone,
Front row: George White, Freddie Lewis, -, -, Danny Smith, - , Tommy Rowles, Smedley Ralph.
Teachers: Ivor Jenkins, Headmaster; Miss Bertha Macleod; Danny Evans.

Aberllechau Infants School. Class 3, 1931

53 children in the class, including: Idwal Parry, Dennis Maundrell, Ken Evans, Ivor Rowlands, Gwyn Cooper, David Gooding, Len Bryant, Tom Evans, Trevor Rowlands, Arthur Willis, Fred Jones, Les Potter, Hugh O'Neill, Leo Evans, Tom Hughes, David Jenkins, Trevor Evans, Idris Morgan, Ronald Thomas, Teify Thomas, Megan Langford, Betty Jones, Rose Jordan, Mary Sweet, Janet Phillips, Beatrice Cull, Ada Pearce, Betty Roberts, Tom Franklyn, Len Gough, George Preece, Haydn Parry, Roy Adams, Dennis Rees, Ivor Jenkins, Reg Mortimer, Sylvia Williams, Alice Jones, Myra Hudd, Betty Smith, Olive Manders, Blodwen Matthews, Haydn Addis, Glyn Evans, Bill Maddern, Ivor Jones, Vic Nelson, Billy Lewis.

Aberllechau Mixed, Standard 6b, 1931

Aberllechau Mixed School Teachers, 1933
Back row (left to right): Len Jones, Tom Davies, G. Thomas, Glenys Wooton, Megan Davies, George Winter
Front row: Thomas Brinley Evans, David Moore, Elsie Jones, Ivor Jenkins, Florence Rowlands,
Goronwy Thomas, Bertha Macleod.

These trips had become a feature of school life now and, in 1930, twenty-five scholars went to London Zoo, while ten children visited Stratford-upon-Avon. The school had another day off in June for the Constitutional Club outing.

Another recorded event was a two-week holiday for the older girls of the mixed school at Pendine Camp, from July 17th to August 4th 1931. This was a new venture, which was led by Miss Ceinwen Williams and Miss Elsie Jones.

118

In March 1932, 30 scholars from Std VII attended the Welsh Book Exhibition in Cardiff, and in May, the scholars were given a tea party by the East Rhondda Unionist Parliamentary Association. Later in June, Sir William James Thomas of Ynyshir gave another tea party for the children.

School trips continued in June, when seven boys and one girl were taken to the G.W.R. works at Swindon, by Miss Florence Rowlands, followed by 25 children visiting Windsor with Miss Rowlands and Mr G. Thomas, and then another 55 pupils off to Bristol Zoo.

In December, the Prince of Wales visited the Rhondda and the school closed for half a day to cheer the visitors!

Changes were taking place in the school premises, with the need for more room. The Std VII boys had classes in Carmel vestry, but there was still overcrowding, so in 1933 two new classrooms were built, which became Std VIIa and Std VIIb girls. This was always known as the New Building.

These were days of unemployment and depression and children of the unemployed were given vouchers to receive boots and shoes free of charge. This was paid for by the Rhondda Boot Fund, set up for that purpose. It was money given and raised by jumble sales and other means in which the teachers themselves took part.

The Duke of Kent and Princess Marie were married in November 1934, which gave the school a day off.

In September of that year, the mixed school recorded 424 pupils present out of 458 on the register and the infants had 251 present. The total seems incredible by today's standards! The following year, 1935, was by contrast quite eventful. The King's Silver Jubilee in May was commemorated with a party for the schoolchildren, given by members of Crawshay Bailey estate trustees. In September, Mr W. E. Morgan became the new headmaster.

A number of schools in the depressed areas of South Wales were adopted by other schools which were not suffering the deprivations of mass unemployment and poverty. Croham Hurst School, South Croydon, adopted Aberllechau. They sent gifts of novelties, clothing and toys that were distributed to the schoolchildren of Aberllechau in December.

Truancy had been a problem in the earlier years, but the education authorities encouraged regular attendances. This sometimes bore fruit and children were presented with a gift for five years' unbroken schooling. Thus, in July, Dorothy Farwell of Danygraig Terrace received a silver watch and fountain pen for five years without a day's absence. On these occasions, local councillors were present and the children were given a half day off to celebrate. Teacher Mr T. B. Evans was a keen sportsman and became a certified swimming instructor. He took interest in the sporting life of the school and encouraged the boys in soccer and swimming. 1936 was the year of sporting success for Aberllechau and, in February, the Porth & District School League team went to Wallasey, near Birkenhead.

The school supplied three boys for the team, which was captained by Trevor Rowlands. Trevor was capped and played for the Wales Schoolboys team. He played in Belfast against Ireland, in Aberdare against England and in Falkirk against Scotland, in the left-back position. The school was very proud of this achievement as Trevor was the first capped player from Aberllechau and they exhibited his cap and jersey for many years. In September of the same year, at a swimming gala, George Gooding, George Harvey, Elwyn Rees, William Isaac and John Williams won a silver cup and six medals. The school timetable was altered in September to accommodate the new *'Radio Broadcasting for Schools'* from the BBC. A relay speaker was set up in Room C and both sections of the school were able to listen, for the first time, to the radio!

In May 1937, the whole school was closed for four days' holiday, to celebrate the succession of Edward VIII. Dorothy Farwell's attendance record increased to 7 years without absence. As a reward, Dorothy received a handbag and the school a half-day's holiday!

Miss Fanny Rowlands had been at the school since before 1913, when records for the mixed school began. In October, she left after 24 years, to get married. She had been a very popular teacher and was remembered by generations of pupils. Mrs Linda Holland (nee Peel), of Pleasant View, remembers her in 1914 as a very young teacher who took an interest in all the girls and their preparations for life in the world of work.

In December 1937, John Williams, George Gooding and Edwin Mason, all Std VII boys, passed their Intermediate Certificate of the Royal Lifesaving Society, at Cardiff Corporation Baths. These were the first successes for any elementary school in the Rhondda. Mr T. B. Evans was their instructor.

March 31st, 1938 was an exciting day for the senior classes and staff who took part in a St. David's Day broadcast from Moriah Chapel, Ynyshir. The chapel organist was one of their teachers, Mr Goronwy Thomas, and as a result of the broadcast, the school received a half-day holiday and a cheque for £1.19s. from the BBC, presented by the conductor, Mr E. T. Lloyd.

A sporting victory in September in the Elementary Schools Swimming Championships brought a silver cup to the school, when George Gooding won the 100 yards free style race for 12-15 year olds in 75 seconds. Another competitor was Edwin Mason in the breast stroke event.

As the threat of war approached, the ARP (Air Raid Precautions) met in the school to practise their drill in the event of hostilities taking place.

1939, the year war broke out, began quietly enough with the children rehearsing for the 'Gymanfa Alawon Gwerin' held in Saron, Ynyshir on St. David's Day. Camping out was highly popular and during this year Mr T. B. Evans accompanied five boys to Rhoose for two weeks, while later in May, Mr T .D. Davies and Mr Len Jones took 28 boys to Ogmore, and Miss Elsie Jones accompanied 28 girls to Gileston camp.

The Ministry of Health closed the Wattstown Park Baths in June due to an outbreak of 'spotted fever' in the district. The war, however, meant preparations continued as the police used the school in the evenings to educate the local population in the use of gas masks. The staff were employed in canvassing and taking a census of accommodation available for evacuated children from areas in danger of air raids.

On September 5th, war was declared and the school was closed to pupils for one week. The teachers were allotted special duties in preparation for the anticipated influx of refugees, and in November, ten children were welcomed into the school – the first of many. There was some good news, however, when David Hughes received a silver watch for 5 years unbroken attendance, together with a fountain pen, presented by the staff. In December of that year, Cynthia Barrow, Std. VI, won the first prize of 10 shillings after writing an essay about her visit to an electricity showroom.

Evacuees continued to arrive during 1940 and, in June, seventeen came from London to be billeted in Wattstown, accompanied by a teacher from the L.C.C., Mrs Richards. Throughout the year, many more arrived at the school, including another teacher, Mr Perkins. Air raids became part of school routine and often disrupted the day, as pupils and staff would evacuate to the air raid shelter, returning after the 'All Clear' siren to resume lessons. The logbook records it took one and a half minutes to clear the school and five minutes to return to classes! Due to the disturbances and loss of sleep caused by these air raid warnings, the school was assembled at 10 a.m. instead of 9 o'clock each day. School life continued, however, and pupils were again presented with watches, pens and certificates for exemplary attendance records. Thomas Hughes and George Farwell (5 years), David and Richard Hughes (5 years), and Dorothy Farwell who had completed almost 8 years.

The Rhondda was bombed in May 1941 and casualties occurred, which resulted in postponement of exams for a week. Another teacher came from Birmingham, Miss Blanche Watterson, but Miss Elsie Jones left to become headmistress of Blaenclydach School after 21 years service in Aberllechau. She was highly regarded as a loyal teacher and well liked by both staff and pupils. Mr J. A. Davies joined the forces and left the school. In May 1943, a fire in Nebo vestry affected the school arrangements for a while, but the School Meals Service began in June when, for the first time, 100 meals were served to the children.

The following year, more evacuees arrived from London and the Midlands. They had a teacher from the L.C.C., Mrs Dawson, who remained only a few months and went back to London with ill health in November. Her replacement was Miss C. K. Cottrell, who was soon replaced by another teacher, Miss J. M. Birchley. Miss Fenwick, the headmistress, retired from the profession and Miss Gladys Jones (Gorwell) became the new headmistress of the Infants School on October 2nd 1944. That same month, Beryl Langford, a pupil of 13 years of age, was killed in an accident with a bus in Ynyshir, while in November, Mr Tom Davies B.A. died suddenly and the whole school attended the funerals. The war still gave reason for the Firewatchers to meet in the school for fire drill.

January 1945 began with heavy snow which kept pupils away and closed the school for a week. The war was coming to a close, and on 8th May, the country rejoiced at the end of hostilities in Europe. The schoolchildren had two days holiday for V.E. Day celebrations. It was not until August 15th that the war in the Far East came to an end, when Japan surrendered. There was a great feeling of relief now that it was over. One of the school's most popular teachers, Mr David Moore, died in

October, aged 59. He had taught at the school for 37 years, with almost 40 years in the Rhondda teaching service. All the staff, pupils, parents and grandparents were deeply saddened by his death, and 30 senior pupils accompanied the staff to attend his funeral.

In December, Noreen King, a pupil, died of Bright's Disease, and once again the school lined the roads in respect.

After the war had ended, evacuees returned home, and Mr J. T. A. Williams returned from service in the RAF to rejoin the school staff. The school settled down to a new routine, which would never be quite the same again. A 13-year-old pupil from Std 7, Betty Easley, died from meningitis in

Ynis Holland and Eufron Jenkins on the V.E. Day 1945 school celebrations.

June 1946. The Sunday School of Bethel went to Barry, and only 146 pupils were left in the whole school. No school that day! This was the year when all schoolchildren became entitled to free milk – one third of a pint.

Teachers at Aberllechau Juniors, July 1945.

Back row: Miss Megan Davies, Ceinwen Bowen, David Moore, Miss Margaret Harris,
Len Jones, Miss Ceinwen Howell
Front row: Megan Roberts, W. R. Morgan, Goronwy Thomas.

Teachers at Aberllechau Juniors, 1947.
Back row: Len Jones, J. T. A. Williams, Goronwy Thomas
Front row: Nan Williams, Ceinwen Howell, W. R. Morgan (Head), Margaret Harris, Megan Davies,

1947 began with prolonged disruption by the weather. The snow began in January and continued to affect the country until March. School attendances were poor for some time as people struggled to come to terms with the low temperatures and blocked roads. Even in March, the school dinners had to be carried from Hillside up to Nebo, due to the slippery conditions.

Although cold weather continued, attendances improved slightly because pupils were often warmer in school than at home, where families were without coal, or the children had no warm winter clothing. In November, the wedding of Princess Elizabeth and the Duke of Edinburgh closed the school for a day, and in September, Miss Agnes E. Jones (Gorwel) retired from teaching, after 30 years at the school.

Royal events in 1948 again gave reason for celebrations, with a free day for the pupils — the Silver Wedding of the King and Queen in April, and the birth of a son to the Princess Elizabeth in November. Field Marshal Viscount Montgomery visited Rhondda in September. Mr W. R. Morgan, the headmaster of the mixed school for 14 years, retired in July. He wrote an emotional report in the school logbook, which spoke of his happy years spent in Aberllechau School. He ended with, 'I shall never forget this day.' Byron Seldon gave a speech of thanks on behalf of the pupils and Sonia Jones presented a bouquet of flowers. The new headmaster was Mr Edwin Parry B.Sc.

The school logbook records two sad items in 1949. In February, a pupil, Richard Morgan of Standard 1, died after an accident involving a bus, while another pupil, Anthony Hughes of Standard 3, died in October. The logbook also records that, in November, a relay wireless was installed in the Junior school. 1950 had little to report, except the sad death in June of Mr J. T. A. Williams, who had entered the forces during the war and returned in 1946 to rejoin the staff of the school.

In January of 1951, 56% of the pupils were away with influenza and a member of staff was suspected of having TB. This resulted in all pupils being X-rayed in a mass radiography scheme designed to fight the disease. The school went on a trip to the Festival of Britain in July, while the reorganising of the Rhondda schools resulted in the Mixed school becoming "Aberllechau Junior Mixed" from September 10th.

This reorganisation also meant that some children now came from another catchment area, and others had to leave the school. 48 boys went to Islwyn and 45 girls went to Ynyshir, while 40 children came to Aberllechau from Ynyshir, namely from Heath Terrace, Standard View and Incline Row.

Aberllechau Junior Mixed School, 1953.
Teacher: Gethin Williams
Back row (left to right): Marion Rees, Geoffrey Simmonds, Maldwyn Evans, Ralph Davies, Michael Ablett
3rd row: Marilyn Uzzell, Bernice Rhys, Brian Mainwaring, Danny Davies, Jeff Evans, Anita Collins, Marion Powell, Hazel Pike
2nd row: Rita Simmonds, Denise McCulloch, Sandra Clee, Mary Atkins, Marlene Davies, Maureen Rees
1st row: Alan Watts, Freddie Jones, Glyn Phelps, Tony Thomas, Susan Rhydderch, Sandra Morgan, Ann Owen, Paul Rhydderch, Malcolm Harries

Aberllechau Infants, 1952.
Headmistress: Miss Gladys M. Jones, and Miss Gwyneth Morris.
Back row (left to right): Gwyn Rickards, David Howells, ?, Roy Evans, Michael Hughes, Graham Harcombe,
? Griffiths, Granville Williams, Mal Palmer, Howard Williams
Middle row: Carol Matthews, Yvonne Howells, Valerie Lloyd, Joan Passey, Bryn Roberts, ?, Irene Harcombe,
Morfydd Hooper, Glenys Llewelyn, Margaret Evans
Front row: Roma King, Anna Thomas, ?, Raymond Hughes, Raymond Easley, Christine Uzzell, Cynthia Davies,
Elaine Down.

Aberllechau Infants, 1952.
Headmistress Miss Gladys M. Jones, and Miss Gwyneth Llewelyn
Back row (left to right): Phillip Maddern, Phillip Scuse, Roy Wedlake, Spencer Wiltshire, ?, Vincent Davies,
David Jones, David Down, Paul Joslin, Chris Williams, Michael Davies
3rd row: Mavis Norton, Donna Stevens, Mavis ?, Gill Ellis, Doreen Harris, Julie Bennett, Christine Robinson,
Pat French, Janice Phelps, Anne Davies
2nd row: Pat Kennedy, Janice Matravers, Janet Rhydderch, Jean Bowen, Christine Gully, Muriel Jones, Gillian Mee,
Grace Makin, Jennifer Davies
Front row: Robert Maddern, Colin Day, ?, Robert Edwards, Dennis Norris, David Allen

Aberllechau Mixed, 1955-56.
Back row (left to right): Brian Cory, Michael Davies, Christopher Jones, David Jones, David Allen, Gareth Williams,
Barrie Hamilton, Michael Davies, Sylvia Evans, Gillian Mee
3rd row: Keith Daniels, Spencer Wiltshire, John Parry, Robin Hammond, Doreen Harris, Gwenda Griffiths,
Valda Jones, Randal Gully, Lionel Langford
2nd row: Grace Makin, Ann Jones, Robert Edwards, Peter Maddern, Colin Dearman, Robert Maddern,
Marilyn Uzzell, Ann Davies, Miss Howell
Front row: Colin Diamond, Ann Owen, Philip Skuse, Christine Gully, Myra Thomas

Aberllechau Juniors, Football Team, 1955-56
Back row (left to right): David Howells, Lionel Langford, Randall Gully, Colin Diamond, Philip Skuse
2nd row: Mr David John Roberts, Christopher Jones, Peter Maddern, Freddie Jones, Spencer Wiltshire, Colin Day,
Mr John Rhys Owens
Front row: Michael Davies, Haydn Howells, Gareth Williams, Glyn Phelps

Wattstown Junior Football Team, circa 1920

Played Ynyshir at Wattstown Park — Wattstown won 6-nil

Back row (left to right): John Kane, ?, David Moore, Morgan Benjamin (referee), Jack Arthur Davies, Tom Thomas, Daniel Hewitt

Middle row: George Thomas, Charles Young, 'Dobbin', John Jones, Evan Morris, 'Billy Bristol'

Front row: W. J. Parry (Bach), Jimmy Phelps, Gough James, Gwyn Jenkins (captain), Gough Ralph, Morgan Rees, Mannie Thomas, Mr Kemp (trainer)

Gwyn Jenkins (captain) scored 5 goals. The captain of Ynyshir was David Mason

Gwyn Jenkins and Charlie Young

In 1952, Mr E. Parry BSc, the headmaster since 1948, moved to Maerdy Junior School, and Miss Ceinwen G. Gwilym became the new headmistress of the 'Junior Mixed'.

The school excursion that year was to St Fagans, Barry, St Athan, Cowbridge, Ewenny and Porthcawl, in June. The King died in February after a long illness.

In 1954, Kenneth George Harris fell on ice in the school yard and lost two front teeth. Heavy snow in January 1955 meant that only 52 children attended the infants school and teachers failed to arrive.

127

Aberllechau School Football Team, 1977-78
Back row (left to right): ?, ?, Richard Philpott, Neil Thorburn, ?, Adrian James.
Middle row: Mansel Mortimer, Anthony Davies, Andrew Thorburn (capt), Mark Jones, Chris O`Brien
Front row: David Pugh, Howard Phillips, Russell Smith.
The unknown players were sent to make up the team from Trehafod Junior School.

Miss Gladys M. Jones, the head of the infants school, retired on March 1st, after 40 years service with the Rhondda Education Authority. Mrs Blanche Richards succeeded her as the new headmistress. In April, the school closed, as the Rhondda Urban District Council became a Borough by Royal Charter.

The logbook for the first time reported a break-in at the school and items were stolen. No thefts had been recorded before this. PC Joslin, however, returned the stolen goods after speaking to the culprit. In 1956, Mansel Owen fell and sprained his ankle and was carried home by Mrs Myra Clarke. It was later discovered that he had broken it! In June, the school XI won the Porth & District Primary Schools League Challenge Cup.

The team was trained and encouraged by teachers Mr Rhys Owens and Mr D. J. Roberts, who were praised for taking such interest in the boys at sport. Eric Rowlands was awarded a certificate and a prize for his essay, entered in the Safety First Essay Competition. Robert Morgan, Paul Vale and Clive Francis received Certificates of Merit.

The caretakers went on strike in October, which meant no fires in the school and no school for the children for a few days. Another flu epidemic, and the infants school rewired for electricity was the main news for 1957.

1958 was celebrated with the Festival of Wales. Some of the local schools combined for a Festival of Song, held in Saron Chapel, Ynyshir. Miss Ceinwen Gwilym, the head of Aberllechau Junior School, conducted the singing. One of the teachers was moved from the Junior School in April 1959, and not replaced. As a result, the classes were reduced from seven to six.

March 2nd 1960, was the celebration of the birth of Prince Andrew, and Michael Osmond fell down the steps and cut his head. The Infants School had a new headmistress, Miss Gwladys Davies, who took over from Miss Blanche Richards in September.

1961 was very routine, with little to report, but 1962 began badly for the Junior School when burst pipes and icy weather closed it for a few days. Later in December, Miss Gertrude Davies B.A. retired after 17 years of faithful service.

1963 had a bad start to the year, with snow and ice which closed the school for most of January and February. The toilets were unusable and there were no school meals or free milk deliveries. The water was shut off and there was no heating for the classrooms.

At the end of the year, work began on the Junior School. A new staffroom and a corridor were built, the cloakrooms were modernised and the ceilings in the main building were lowered. This work continued into 1964, and in July of that year Miss Ceinwen Gwilym retired as head of the Junior School after 12 years' service at Aberllechau. Mr E. M. Roberts became the new headmaster.

There was little to report in 1965, except that Jennifer Welch fell in the gym and sprained her wrist.

On March 28th, 1966, the school was shocked to receive the sad news that Miss G. Davies, the headmistress of the Infants School, had died in Llwynypia Hospital of a heart attack. She had been the head for only six years. The next day, Miss Gwyneth Morris took over as temporary head teacher.

The logbook records an illegal entry into the school in May. One shilling and three pence was taken from the cupboard in the Infants School, and PC Ray Smith conducted an interview at the school. A pupil, Julie Vale, broke a finger playing in the school yard. In July, Miss Olwen Morris was appointed the new head teacher.

Mr Alan Rowe, who began teaching in the Junior School in 1966, took Std 4 for a tour of the National Colliery in June 1967. The colliery closed the following year. There is no connection between the two incidents! The following year was uneventful, but big changes took place in 1969. Mrs Olwen Morris retired as head of the Infants School in April. The two schools became one, known as Aberllechau Junior & Infants School, on 3rd September, 1969. Mr Albert Snell became the head of the Infants and Mr E. M. Roberts remained as the head of the Juniors.

Aberllechau Mixed School, 1957-58 and 1959-60

Both classes contain mainly the same children, the earlier group aged about 7 years, and the older group aged about 10.

The teachers are Miss Megan Davies and Mr Gethin Williams.

The pupils include: Ronald Spence, Linda Owens, Moira Evans, Sheila Maundrell, Susan Thomas, Janet Collins, Geoffrey Collins, Angela Evans, Barbara Llewelyn, Carol John, Steven Evans, Lynne Meddick, Cheryl Pearce, John Evans, Ronald Rees, Janet Edwards, Ann Jones, Yvonne Lock, Phillip Matravers, Pauline Jones, Donald Evans, Janet Hughes, Susan Matthews, Ian Mays, Tony Jones, Mansel Owen, Donald Evans. Christine Withers, Sandra Powell, Linda Williams, Howell Jenkins.

Aberllechau School Juniors, 1959
Back row (left to right): Sandra Withers, Janice Evans, Peter Fitzgerald. Paul Greedy, Derek Weaver, Terry O`Brien,
Ralph Davies, Colin Harvey, Russell Craven, Paul Vale
3rd row: Marsden Casey, Glenys Llewelyn, Paul Joslin, Eileen Thomas, Granville Williams, Pamela Edwards,
Howard Williams, Howard Mann
2nd row: Meirion Folks, Maureen Rowlands, Sheila Ward, Jennifer Price, Yvonne Jones,
Yvonne Lewis, Christine Uzzell
Front row: Hilary Mee, Margaret O`Brien, Pat Smith, Elaine Down, Janice Morgan, David Pugh
Teacher: David John Roberts

Mrs Megan Morris had been a member of staff at the school for 29 years. She retired from teaching in July, 1971, when she was sadly missed. Two years later, in July 1973, Mr E. M. Roberts, head of the Juniors, also retired after 43 years service. Mr Albert Snell, head of the Infants, became the head teacher of the whole school.

1974 began with a coal shortage, which closed the school for the first three months. In March of that year, a young pupil, Cliff Dwyer, died. A group of older children went to Holland in April, accompanied by Mr Colin Harvey and Mr Alan Rowe. The records state that on 27th November 1974, the school was closed for the International Rugby Match, New Zealand v Wales. Very little is recorded during the next few years, apart from the movement of teachers and other routine matters. New outdoor toilets were built in 1976 and, in June 1977, work began on new indoor toilets. Mr Snell moved to Ton Pentre Junior School in 1980, and Mr Mansel Llewelyn became the new headmaster. Anthony Haines was awarded a prize for the photograph which he had entered into *'The History of the Rhondda'* competition. 1981 was the year of the wedding of Princess Diana and Prince Charles and a party for the pupils took place in the school. In May, Kevin Brain and Stephen Atkins received trophies as members of the football team playing in the District League.

Aberllechau Mixed.
Back row (left to right): Miss Megan Davies, Kelvin Stone, ?, Stephen Addison, Gareth Jenkins, Steven Jenkins,
Steven Bird, Alan Woodward. Mr E. M. Roberts, headmaster
3rd row: Elaine Parmee, Pam Jones, Julie Jones, Pauline Ward, Anne Down, Anwen Davies.
2nd row: Janet Owens, Meryl Harries, Cheryl Bennett, Gillian Turner, Angela Davies, Ruth Bosley, Lyn Cameron
Front row: Stephen Davies, Gareth Williams, ?, Graham Jones, ?

The following year, Mr Alan Rowe left after 16 years at Aberllechau, to become deputy head at a school in Williamstown, while Mr Colin Harvey left after 13 years service, for a similar position at Penygraig.

1983 was a year of sporting success, as the school won the Rhondda Fach Junior Schools Football League, something not achieved since 1968. The school team also shared the honour of League Champions. One of the pupils, Dean Philpott, played for the Mid Glamorgan Schools against Gwent Schools.

On December 21st, 1984, Miss Gwyneth Morris retired after more than 37 years service. She began her teaching career in 1947 as a nursery assistant, and during the following years became a qualified teacher and deputy head. The logbook records that her contribution to the school was 'inestimable'. A party was held at the school, with a large cake, to celebrate her 60th birthday. She was presented with gifts from the pupils and parents who remembered her from *their* school days, and from the staff. Sadly, Miss Morris died suddenly in February 1986, less than two years after her retirement.

Infants School, 1966-67
Teachers: Miss Beryl Thomas and Miss Dorothy Bennett
Back row (left to right): Mark Bryant, Brian Kirby, David Owen, Ian Baker, Wayne Phillips,
Julian Davies, Malcolm Haines
3rd row: ?, Paul Stone, Frankie Warner,
2nd row: Cheryl Downs, Lynne Powell, Christine Jones, Pauline?, Meryl Wiltshire, Andrea England, Linda Osmond, ?
Front row: Alan Evans, Donna Reed, Beryl Francis, Christine Long, Keith Shepherd

Infants School, 1967 — Harvest Festival
Back row (left to right): ?, Lee Niblett, Clive Langford, ?, David Davies, ?, Lyndon Baker, Denzil Lawrence,
David James, David Stewart, Martin Mays, Mark Jones, Jeff Simmons
Front row: Richard Trow, Debbie Phelps, Karen Davies, Alison Richards, Gerald Williams, ?, Gaynor Llewelyn,
Wendy Hopkins, Susan Parry, Debra Bird, Mandy Price.

Infants School, 1968-1969
Teachers: Miss Beryl Thomas and Mrs Olwen Morris (Head)
Back row (left to right): John Williams, Brian Kirby, Timothy Murphy, Jeff Simmons, Wayne Phillips,
Martin Mays, Martin Jenkins
3rd row: Julian Davies, Malcolm Haynes, Christopher Matravers, Ian Baker, David Owen, Carl Warner
2nd row: Sharon Lloyd, Jacqueline Williams, Meryl Wiltshire, Lynne Powell, Christine Long,
Andrea England, Cheryl Downs
Front row: Mark Bryant, Linda Osmond, Gaynor Llewelyn, Mandy Price, Debbie Phelps, David Ellis

In 1987, the school reached its Centenary Year. Central heating was installed in April. June was the chosen date to celebrate the first 100 years. During the week of 22nd to the 26th, the staff and pupils dressed up in Victorian costume. The children's uniforms were made from a pattern supplied by St Fagans Museum. The children enjoyed having lessons from that era and playing games which their great-grandparents would have played. The school held a party and enjoyed a centenary cake on Tuesday. The people of the village were able to see the records of the school and enjoy concerts given by staff and pupils. The exhibition of memorabilia remained open to the public for two weeks. Thus ended the first 100 years of Aberllechau School.

1988 saw the formation of the Parents' Group, which held its first meeting in May. The introduction of school uniforms had begun the previous year, but did not really get going until 1988. Miss Beryl Thomas, nursery assistant, retired in April and Mrs Eleanor Morgan was appointed deputy head. Lead was stolen from the roof and water entered three classrooms, which prevented them being used.

Mr Mansel Llewelyn retired in July 1992 after 12 years as head teacher and Mr Keith Williams took his position on 7th September 1992. For a large part of 1994, the school was disrupted with workmen building a new kitchen.

Aberllechau Junior School, 1975 — St David's Day
Standing: David Davies, Mary Cameron, Jonathan Davies, Lyndon Baker, Neil Dudson
Seated: Christopher Wilton, David Vivian

This was completed in July and the children were fed in the school for the first time, with its own new kitchen. Nebo vestry had been the school canteen for many years. A street party was held in the school yard in May 1995 to celebrate 50 years since V.E. Day.

Aberllechau School, standing as it does at the centre of the village, has always felt the pulse of the community that surrounds it. The highs and the lows, the bad and the good times were always reflected in the life of the school. It is a barometer of what happened in the community. While the school records these changes, they were never allowed to interfere with, or detract from, the working of the school.

Indeed, the school always rose above these challenges and maintained its high standards of education, while adapting to the problems of the day. The success of education in any generation has always depended on the quality and commitment of the staff. This has always been true of Aberllechau, and continues today in the 21st century. Many will be grateful for the time spent in Aberllechau School and the help and encouragement of the teachers over the years.

Aberllechau School Brass Ensemble, March 1973 — St David's Day Celebrations
(left to right): David Davies, Julian Davies, Lyndon Baker, Ian Baker

Centenary Celebrations in Aberllechau School, 1987
Mr Mansel Llewelyn was the headmaster

Centenary, 1987

The school held a week of celebrations and gave concerts which the parents could enjoy, an exhibition of memorabilia, and the school records were opened for the community to see. The staff and children dressed in uniforms which were similar to those their grandparents may have worn 100 years ago.

ACADEMIC SUCCESSES

This is a list of academic successes as recorded in the school logbook. Unfortunately, not every year was recorded and after 1952, no names were listed at all.

July 1924 — Passes to Entrance Scholarship Exams for Higher Education

John Macintyre, Vera West, Violet Wiltshire, Frances Evans, Maggie Griffiths, Leonard Bateman.

May 1936 — 10 out of 13 passes

Trevor Phillips, Elsie Owen, Mary Wiltshire, Trevor Gwilliam, Margaret Jones, Muriel D. Rees, Myra Nicholls, Pearl Bateman, Rachel Rees, Bronwen M. Davies.

June 1937 — 7 out of 10 passes, no names recorded.

June 1938 — 12 out of 14 passes

Jennet Phillips (275 marks — Top girl in the Rhondda). Edith Weston, Blodwen Matthews, Bernard Thompson, Rosemary Orr, Beryl Morris, Thomas G. Cooper, Leslie Willis, Trevor Evans, Betty Smith, Clifford Milliner, Thomas Davies.

Special Exam for Form 3 Porth County. Success for Eiddwen Miles and Betty Price.

June 1939

11 out of 11 passes in Scholarship Exams, and 2 out of 4 for Junior Tech

Ada Stone (8th), Walter Lovering, Dawn Jenkins, Glenys Finnear, Emlyn Cameron, Margaret M. Thomas, Fred Yeoman, Jean R. Bateman, Erica James, Ken Thompson, Morfydd Davies

Junior Tech: Haydn Addis, Thomas J. Evans.

June 1940 — 6 out of 8 passes

Olwen Griffiths, Agnes V. Hughes, Catherine E. Griffiths, Joan Morris, Ivor Smith, Arthur Viner.

June 1941 — 15 out of 20 passes

Mansel Finnear, Roderick Hutchings, Margaret Jenkins, Gwyneth Jenkins, Gordon Dyer, Vernon John, Thelma Lloyd, William D. Bateman, David Uzzell, Irene Rowlands, Vera Collins, Phoebe Evans, Doreen Lovering, Rosanna Ball.

June 1942 — 15 successes

Ronald Williams, Ivor Hughes, Elizabeth Rees, Lillian Hutchings, Gordon Evans, Patricia Wilding, Clifford Maundrell, Glynmor Cooper, Ernest Orr, Beryl Johnson, Thomas Pritchard, Donald James, Gerald Thomas, Margaret Jones, Lillian Ball, John Thistlewood (evacuee).

July 1943 — 11 passes

Doreen Parmee, Betty Jenkins, D. J. Hughes, Jean Macey, Margaret Davies, Ron Lovering, Thom Thomas, Eben Phillips, Ronald Maddern, Hugh Barrow, Geoffrey Ford.

1944 / 1945 — No Records

June 1946 — 6 passes for Secondary School, and 2 passes for Junior Tech

Gordon Rowlands, Lorna Manders, Maldwyn Jones, John Evans, William Kirby, Rosa Davies.

Junior Tech: Dennis Hughes (2nd in Rhondda), Brian Bateman (6th).

June 1947 — 10 passes for Secondary School

Catherine Robbins, Ann Wiltshire, Ynis Holland, David Thompson, Ronald Lewis, Wendy Jenkins, Janice Evans, Gareth Rees, Iris Beryl Jones, Shirley Finnear.

June 1948 — 19 out of 20 passes

The first 12 to Porth County, and the remainder to Ferndale.

Brian Stephens, William John, Brian Wiltshire, John Davies, Pat Maddern, Joyce Powell, Elizabeth Crewe, Ruby King, Sheila Gully, Alex Smith, Pat Morgan, Derek Lye, Irene Richards, Gwenda Owen, Haydn Davies, John Harris, Ellen Thomas, David Jones, Thomas Jones.

June 1949 — 9 passes

Gillian Evans, Brian John, Sheila James, Idris Owen, Pat Jones, Edith Clements, Shirley Miles, Pat Pike, Brian Rees.

July 1950 — 8 passes for Secondary School, and 3 passes for Tech

Brian Bean, Haydn Robinson, Howard Thomas, Alun Evans, Anne Stroud, Leonard Lewis, Michael Ricketts, Glyndwr Evans.

Technical Entrance:

Melvyn Thomas, William Shewell, Raymond Haynes.

June 1951
14 passes for Secondary School, and 1 pass for Technical School

Colin Parmee, David Gully, Robert King, Michael Evans, Myra Crewe, Anthony Lewis, Melissa Jolley, Mary J. Davies, Pat Mainwaring, Joan Hopkins, Marilyn Owen, David Davies, Gillian Kingsbury, Kay Phillips.

Tech - Glyndwr Davies.

July 1952 — The first 6 to Porth County

Anne Hopkins (1st in Rhondda), Margaret Rowlands (2nd), Anthony Evans, Marilyn Davies, June Jones, Raymond Minett, Ronald Ricketts, Ann Rees, Diane R. Davies, Sonia D. Jones, William M. Gooding, Gladys E. Lye, Allan Coles, Islwyn Thomas, Lillian Wiltshire, Anne Trow, Eira G. Rogers, Kenneth J. Haynes, Danny Smith, Brian Richards.

These are all the recorded names. Many more passes were recorded but no names given.

The following list consists of teachers, both qualified and unqualified, trainees, nursery assistants, pupil teachers, students on teaching practice, those given a bursary, supply, remedial, and temporary teachers. I have simply included the date at which they are recorded as having started at the school, in whatever capacity.

THE INFANTS SCHOOL

1887 Mrs W. I. Griffiths, headmistress, 1887 to 1889.
Miss Elizabeth Gronnow, headmistress, 1889 to 1906.
Miss Mary Jane Morgan — entered Mixed School in 1889.

1889 Miss Esther Gibbon

1892 Miss Mary Owens, Miss Annie Thomas, Miss Margaret E Davies.

1894 Miss Elizabeth Murton Martyn.

1896 Miss Elizabeth J. Powell.

1905 Miss Ellen Mary Selwood

1906 to 1922. Miss Elizabeth Phillips, headmistress

1907 Miss Elizabeth E. Rees, Miss Bronwen Williams, Miss Ethel Davies. Miss Elizabeth Williams.

1910 The school is extended and the new building becomes the Infants.

1917 Miss Gwladys M. Jones, Miss Mary Stephens, Miss Mary Rosser, Miss Anne Wellcome, Miss Rachel Keast, Miss Katie Watts, Miss Alice Jones, Miss Agnes Jones, Miss Lillian Hanham, Miss Margaret Thomas, Miss Lilwen Richards, Miss Katie Hughes.

1919 Miss Jane Parry, Miss Margaret E. Powell, Miss Lillian Agnes Taylor, Miss Lillian Richards, Miss Francis Ethel Mearles.

1922 Miss Elizabeth Fenwick, headmistress, 1922 to 1944.
Miss Olwen Williams.

1923 Miss Margaret M. H. Sidney, Miss Hannah Davies.

1924 Miss Mary A. Davies, Miss Mary Maud Bryant, Miss Gladys Colburn, Miss Margaret Selina Powell, Miss Hilda May Ellis, Miss Doris Roberts, Miss Elizabeth Jane Davies.

1925 Miss Olive Gwendoline Shelley, Miss Margaret Lewis.

1927 Miss Winifred Annie Baiter, Miss Eirwen Jenkins, Miss Phyllis Evans. Miss Gwendoline Phillips, Miss Hannah Mary Bowen.

1928 Miss Margaret Mary Edwards.

1929 Miss Lily Lewis, Miss Margaret Anne Jones

1930 Miss Sarah Jane Davies.

1932 Miss Edna May Edwards, Miss Sarah Jane Jones.

1933 Miss Mary Irene Jones.

1935 Miss Sarah Thomas.

1937 Miss Hannah M. Davies.

1938 Miss Catherine Kane, Miss Gladys Jones (left for headship in Trehafod).

1939 Miss Nellie Davies.

1940 Miss Kitty Reeves, Mrs Richards (Evacuees' Teacher from LCC).

1941 Miss Nesta Jones.

1942 Miss Agnes E. Jones.

1943 Miss Gwyneth Llewelyn.

1944 Miss Fenwick retired from the teaching profession.
Miss Gladys M. Jones returns to become the new headmistress.
Mrs Dawson (LCC) replaces Mrs Richards as Evacuees' Teacher.
Miss C. K. Cottrell takes over from Mrs Dawson.
Miss J. M. Birchby replaces Miss Cottrell.

1945 Mrs Annie May Barrett

1946 Miss Glenys Rosina Evans, Miss Ethel Maud Evans, Miss Nan Williams.

1947 Miss Glenys R. Trow, Miss Gwyneth Morris, Miss Audrey Ruttley, Miss Cornelia A. Edwards, Miss M. A. Lewis, Miss Agnes E. Jones retired from the teaching profession.

1948 Mrs Mary Ann Lewis, Miss Margaret A. Jones retires after 40 years in the profession.

1951 Miss Novello Edwards.

1952 Miss Muriel Ella Edmunds.

1953 Miss June Jones, Mrs Octavia Slade, Miss Gaynor Ann Lloyd.

1954 Miss Joan D. Owen, Miss Olwen Howells, Miss Myra Clarke,
Miss Joyce Williams.

1955 Miss Gladys M. Jones retires after 40 years in the teaching profession.
Mrs Blanche Richards becomes the new headmistress.

1956 Miss Pat Maddern.

1957 Miss Eirwen J. Phillips.

1960 Miss Blanche Richards retires from the teaching profession.
Mrs Gwladys Davies becomes the new headmistress.

1961 Miss Margaret Hopkins.

1963 Mrs Cynthia Mainwaring (nee Saunders), Miss Carol Kendall.

1964 Miss Gillian Evans, Miss Beryl Thomas, Miss Ann Humphreys.

1966 Mrs Gwladys Davies died suddenly of a heart attack in hospital.
Mrs Olwen Morris appointed as new Headmistress.
Miss Dorothy Bennett.

1967 Miss Gwyneth L. Evans, Miss G. Morgan.

1968 Mrs Velma Carder.

1969 Mrs Olwen Morris resigned as headmistress.

The Infants School joined with the Mixed on September 6th 1969, to become one, known as Aberllechau Junior & Infants School.

THE MIXED SCHOOL

No records exist for the Mixed School until 1913. When the school was extended in 1910, Mr Daniel Phillips became the headmaster. There is no information regarding a previous head teacher. It may have been Miss E. Phillips, who was listed as the head of the Infants.

The staff are listed below -

1913 Mr Daniel Phillips, headmaster, Mr D. Evans, Mrs Humphreys, Miss Griffiths, Miss Florence Rowlands, Mr Rees, Miss Catherine M. Williams, Mr D. Moore, Miss Alice A. Jones.

1914 Mr Howells, Mr Thomas Davies, Miss Hannah Jane Griffiths.

1915 Mr D. J. Maidment, Mr D. J. Evans, Miss Jennie Price.

1916 Mr Idwal Evans, Miss Dorothy G. Jones, Mr Jack Arthur Davies, Miss Maggie Jones.

1918 Mrs Humphreys.

1919 Mr Edwin Fielding.

1920 Miss Elsie Jones, Miss Minnie Shibko, Miss Olwen Morris.

1922 Mr E. V. Dodd.

1923 Mr Ivor Day.

1924 Mr Thomas Brinley Evans, Mr Oswald Morgan.

1928 Mr D. Phillips retires as head of the Mixed School. Mr Ivor R. Jenkins is appointed as the new headmaster. Miss Bertha Macleod Jones, Miss Ceinwen Williams, Mr Goronwy Thomas.

1929 Mr Leonard Jones, Mr Irving Cooper, Miss Mary Thomas, Mr Thomas D. Davies, B.A.

1930 Miss Llewela M. Voyle, Miss Mary Gwyneth Hughes, Miss Megan E. Davies.

1931 Mr George Winter, Miss Glenys Morwen Wooton, Miss Nellie Thomas.

1933 Miss Gwyneth M. Powell.

1934 Miss Nellie Clapworthy.

1935 Mr Ivor Jenkins retired. Mr W. R. Morgan is appointed as the new headmaster.

1936 Mr Cyril Arthur Milliner.

1937 Mr Gwynfryn Pugh Evans, Mr Glyndwr B. Brown, Mr Royston Wiltshire, Miss Fanny Rowlands left to get married.

1939 Miss Burgess, Mr Owen Grey Roberts.

1940 Mrs Richards, LCC, Evacuees' Teacher, Mr Perkins, LCC, Evacuees' Teacher.

1941 Mr Trevor Phillips, Miss A. R. Thomas, Miss Blanche Watterson, Birmingham E.A. Evacuees' Teacher, Miss Elsie Jones leaves after 21 years for a position of headship in Blaenclydach. Miss Megan Elunid Jones, Birmingham E.A. Evacuees' Teacher. Mr J. T. A. Williams joins the forces. Miss M. M. Harris, Miss Thornley, M. A.

1942   Mrs Richards returns to London, Mrs Grimsdale, Mr D. L. Day.

1943   Miss M. James, Mrs B. Owen

1944   Mr Thomas Davies, B.A. dies suddenly. Miss Doreen Morgan.

1945   Miss Ceinwen Howell, Miss G. Davies, Mr D. G. Moore dies after 37 years on staff.

1946   Mr John Elwyn Thomas. Mr J. T. A. Williams returns after war service. Miss Nan Williams transferred from Infants.

1947   Mr Gethin Williams.

1948   Mr W. R. Morgan retires after 14 years as head of the Mixed School. Mr Ivor Parry, B.Sc. appointed new headmaster. Mr William Harold Blake.

1949   Miss Mair Johns.

1950   Mrs H. E. Daniels, Mr J. T. A. Williams died.

1951   Mr Hugh Noel Davies.

1952   Mr I. Parry moves to Maerdy in July. Miss Ceinwen G. Gwilym as new headmistress. Mr Kenneth T. Dorrington.

1953   Mr Goronwy I. Thomas and Mr Len Jones retired in August. Mr David John Roberts, Mr John Rhys Owens, Mr Ebenezer Phillips.

1957   Mrs E. Macnamara.

1958   Mrs A. N. Morgan, Mrs Marion V. Jones.

1959   Mrs Ceridwen Evans, Mrs M. G. Saywood, Miss Ann Hopkins.

1960   Mr. Alan Evans.

1962   Miss Pat Rowlands. Miss Gertrude Davies, B.A. retired after 17 years on staff.

1963   Mr R. A.Trotman.

1964   Miss Ceinwen G. Gwilym retires after 12 years as head of Mixed School. Mr E. M. Roberts becomes new headmaster. Miss Ann Humphreys.

1965   Miss A. Anthony, Miss V. Puckett, Miss M. Wiltshire.

1966   Mr Alan Rowe.

1967   Miss Vilma Davies.

1968   Mr Edward G. James

1969   Miss Margaret Jones, Miss Rosemary Davies, Mr Colin Harvey, Mr Ceri Morse.

1970   Mrs N. Phillips, Miss Wendy Rees, Miss Jane Kirkham, Mr Gareth Williams, Miss Gillian Griffiths, Miss Wendy Morris.

1971   Mrs Megan Morris retired after 29 years on staff. Miss I. L. Carroll.

1972   Miss Sylvia Leatherby, Miss Flora Smith, Miss Margaret Swain, Miss I. Clement.

1973   Mr E. M. Roberts retired after 43 years service. Mr Albert Snell, new headmaster. Mrs L. Bevan, Mr Michael David Thomas.

1974   Miss Crewe, Miss Susan Mary Jones, Mrs Lynne Rowe, Mrs Davina Williams, Mrs A. Morgan, Mrs M. A. Lewis, Mr G. P. Williams, Miss J. Turley, Mr J. Jones.

1975 Mrs Butler, Mrs J. Thomas, Miss Jane Elias, Mrs Eleanor Morgan.

1976 Miss Diane Wendy Rees, Mrs Karen Griffiths, Mrs I. Matthews, Mrs Ann Blake, Mr D. Rees, Miss Karen Sian Price, Miss Beryl Thomas, Miss Gwyneth Morris, deputy head, Mrs Caroline Doe, Mrs D. Williams, Miss Elizabeth Faulkner, Mrs V. M. Snell, Miss L. Thomas, Mrs G. Port.

1977 Miss Ann Evans, Mrs French, supply teacher, Mrs Flannery, Mr Ken Jones.

1978 Mrs Rees, Mr Brian Davies, Mrs Christine Protheroe, Mrs. Norma Phillips.

1979 Mrs G. Cowley, Miss Susan Laskey, Miss Susan Fletcher, Mr D. K. Thomas, Mrs Pat Steadman, Miss Judith Rodgers.

1980 Miss Sally Ann Treadwell, Mr Albert Snell left for Ton Pentre Junior School. Mr Mansel Llewelyn became new headmaster. Mrs V. Hobson.

1981 Mr Thomas Batan, Miss Susan Todd Jones, Miss Wendy Edwards, Mrs R. Viner, Mrs J. Wilde, Mrs Vanstone, Mrs Karen Collins.

1982 Mrs K. Griffiths, Miss Matthew, Miss J. James, Mrs S. Bunny. Mr Alan Rowe left to become deputy head after 16 years in this school. Mr Colin Harvey left to become deputy head after 13 years here.

1983 Mrs J. Sully, Miss Suzanne Sykes.

1984 Mrs A. Foster, Mrs Joy Bishop, Miss Gwyneth Morris retires after over 37 years.

1985 Mrs Jeanne V. Davies becomes deputy head.

1986 Miss Gwyneth Morris dies. Mrs Ann Cook.

1987 School Centenary Week, June 22nd to June 26th.
Mrs Dacey, Mrs P. Mullen, Mrs Sheila Pratton, Miss C. Ingham, Mrs Powell, Miss Faith Adams, Mrs Alice Evans.

1988 Miss Lorna Rye.

1989 Mr Vaggers, Miss Beryl Thomas retires.

1990 Mrs Eleanor Morgan becomes deputy head. Mrs Angela Newall, Miss Lyn Froud.

1991 Mr C. Davies.

1992 Mrs Roberts, Mrs C. Phillips retired after long service. Mr Mansel Llewelyn retires after 12 years as head teacher. Mr Keith Williams becomes new headmaster. Mrs Helen Davies, Miss A James, Miss S. Davies, Miss C. Henshaw.

1993 Miss H. Cuff, Miss A. Jones, Mrs Blight.

1994 Mrs L. Mealing, Miss I. Downey, Miss S. Smith, Mrs Susan Evans.

1995 Mrs P. Lewis, Miss Jayne Price, Miss A. Davies, Mrs Bevan, Miss C. Loin, Mrs D. Davies, Miss Natalie Poole.

1996 Mrs A. Morgan, Miss Kelly Rowans, Miss R. Aldridge, Miss R. Evans.

1998 Miss S. Connell, Miss R. Lewis.

1999 Miss D. Griffiths , Miss L. Jones, Miss Lindsay Holland.

2000 Miss Bonnie Harley, Miss C Montague.

144

Shops and Businesses

During the lifetime of the village, as many as thirty or more shops have existed in Wattstown. Most of these were front rooms opened as a means of making a living, for those who were widows, or families whose breadwinner could no longer work in the pit because of ill-health. There were no social or sickness benefits in those days, only 'parish relief', and many people were very poor, without means of supporting their family. Many of these 'front rooms' sold very basic commodities, often home-made; 'toffee dabs', 'toffee apples', 'sweets', 'spanish root' 'liquorice sticks', paraffin and sand. Sand was used for scouring and covering stone floors. Carpets and 'lino' were beyond the means of most people.

There were other shops, of course, which sold everything you could need: butchers, bakers, drapers, grocers, dairies, general stores (anything), shoe shops, fish & chip shops, barber shops, cobblers, the Post Office and the doctor's surgery.

I have listed all those in living memory, as a record of how it used to be.

*Mrs Ann Evans (Mamgu) outside her shop at 18 Aberllechau Road, circa 1903,
with her daughters Phoebe and Rhoda, sisters to 'Vaughan Evans the Milk'.*

*William Day's first shop opened in 1903, at 19 Aberllechau Road. Notice the newsboard, mentioning the
'Eight Hour Act' which was introduced in 1909.*

146

ABERLLECHAU ROAD

No. 2 (Glenview) Florence Kittley's front room shop in 1920.

No. 7 This was a greengrocer's shop, kept by Thomas Brown and his family of six, from Cornwall, in the 1890's. The building changed hands several times, becoming in turn a greengrocers and Mr Haggett's shoe shop.

No. 7a A greengrocer's shop kept in 1891 by a widow, Ann Evans, from Neath. She had 3 children and 2 lodgers. (12 people in a family was quite common and large families were well known in our communities.) This eventually became the 'Cambrian Stores', owned and managed by Mr Powell, who lived in 'The Villa' in Hillside Terrace. In 1919, the building was purchased by the Mid-Rhondda Cooperative Society, who already owned premises in Ynyshir. Due to the expanding population, 'Cambrian Stores' became the Cooperative shop in Wattstown.

One report of the Society reads : *'.. in order to relieve the great congestion at the Ynyshir branch, we have purchased premises at Wattstown during the new half year (1919) at a cost of £400. We have transferred over 300 members from Ynyshir branch. Only groceries and provisions are being sold at present. Other departments will be opened.'*

In 1934, the two buildings became one, with the addition of a butchery department, where Jim Davies worked.

Here are some names of those who worked in Wattstown Co-op since it began:

Betty Ellis (nee Richards)	Bill Morgan
Glyn Jones	Tom Davies
Dilwyn Davies	Mel Morgan
Jim Davies (Butcher)	Freddie Morgan
Elaine Moulds	Norman Hadfield
Betty Southcombe	Ray England
Edwina Stuart	Sheila Westacott
Ivan James	Gwyneth Keen
Rosie Davies	Cynthia Barnett
Reggie Bunn	Joan James
Carol Williams	Lynne Addis
Susan Bates	Nicola Moses
Les Bateman	

The Cooperative finally closed with the restructuring of the Cooperative movement in 1989. Mr & Mrs John Parry took ownership of the 'Kop' for a few years, until John's sad death meant that the building never regained its place in the community and was finally demolished in April 1999.

The Reynolds Family, circa 1910   Margaret, Annie, Eben, David, Jennet, Sal and, seated, William.

Jennet was the daughter of David Lewis, who had built the slaughterhouse on Aberllechau Road. These were among the very first people to settle in Cwtch in the 1880s. She was one of the founder members of Calfaria in 1894, and some of the family remained connected with the chapel until it closed in 1969. Eben had come from a farming family in Carmarthenshire, and he and Jennet opened a butcher's shop in Aberllechau Road at No. 33. Annie became Mrs Parry, the mother of Collwyn Parry, and Sal was the wife of Dan Phillips the Milk.

*'Days' shop at 35 Aberllechau Road. William Day moved here in 1912.
In the photograph, left to right, are: Mr Boon the barber, the boy is unknown, William Day, Mr. Davey
and a drayman from the Butchers Arms.*

*'The Tuppers Boys Club' who met in the room above 'Days' shop in the 1920s and 1930s.
This studio photograph includes Morris Thomas, George King, and Will Stroud.*

The last day and the end of an era. Dolly Day, Evelyn Maddern, Roy Wiltshire and Madge Wiltshire stand outside on the final day of trading as 'Days' in 1983

Howard Clanfield, sub-postmaster, at 23 Aberllechau Road, 1999

The end of an era as the Cooperative is finally demolished in 1999.

No. 9   In the early 1900s, John Rowe kept a butcher's shop, which was taken over in the 1920's by Anne Haycock, who continued to trade as a butcher. Eventually, it became part of the Cooperative as a fruit and vegetable shop. Mr Rowe also kept a wooden building in Ynyshir, behind Penuel Chapel, known as 'Rowe's Dance Hall.'

No. 9a Mrs Jones, the sister of Evan Rees, boot repairer, kept a fruit and vegetable shop, sharing the premises with her brother in the 1920s. It later became a general store, with Mr Boseley as shopkeeper, and eventually it was taken over by Mr. Crewe.

No. 12 After 1901, this became the Post Office with Job Hoskins as sub-postmaster. It remained a Post Office for many years under David Evans, and later with his daughter, Margaret Evans, known as 'Maggie the Post'. She retired in 1968, when the Post Office was moved to other premises.

No. 18 A greengrocers, kept by Mrs Phoebe Ann Evans, the mother of Mr Vaughan Evans the milk and grandmother of Phoebe Morgan, Bryn Terrace.

No. 19 William Day, a survivor of the 1905 colliery explosion, opened his first shop here in 1903.

No. 20 Having moved next door, Mr. Day fitted shop windows into these premises. It was a general store. He later moved to No. 35, when No. 20 was taken over by Mrs Meredith and her daughter, Rene, who played the organ and piano in Calfaria Chapel.

No. 22 Mr W. J. Wells's fish and chip shop was here during the twenties.

No. 23 During the 1950s and 1960s, this was a chemist shop and pharmacy, owned by Mr Haydn Schofield. The chemist shop was originally opened by Dr Ernest Orr, with Mrs Eveleyn Clifford as pharmacist. Being next door to the surgery, it was very convenient for the patients! During the war years 1940-1945, an Italian family lived there – Mr. & Mrs. Dedino, who sold ice-cream from a cart! Dr Orr and family returned to Ireland and Haydn Schofield moved his business to John Street, Porth. The premises became the Post Office, with Mrs Linehan as postmistress. In 1991, Mr Howard Clanfield took over as postmaster.

No. 24 This was, at one time, Dr Orr's waiting room, with his surgery at the rear.

No. 25 In the 1890s, this was the Post Office, kept by the Reverend Morgan Humphrey Jones, who later built 'Gorwel', in Pleasant View. It became a house and surgery in 1901, first for Dr Davies and later for Dr Orr and family.

No. 26 The first inhabitants of No. 26, in the 1890s, were David Lewis and his family, from Cymmer. He opened a butcher's shop and was instrumental in building a slaughterhouse on the site opposite - where Calfaria garden now stands. It changed in later years, first to a dairy, kept by Mr. Hopkins, who

152

Margaret, Jason and Nicola outside 'His and Hers' hairdressers, at 26a Aberllechau Road, circa 2000

M.S. Motors, body repairers and paint sprayers, circa 2000

Looking down on 'Dunnings' and 'Travis Perkins' on the small industrial estate, circa 2000

*The old colliery site, the home of a number of businesses that have come and gone over the years.
The building is now used by Peacocks as a warehouse.*

154

also collected small coal in a cart, and was then taken over by Mr Thomas. It eventually became a fish and chip shop run by Dilys Davy, who was a sister to Muriel Rhydderch. In the 1980s it became a Chinese takeaway, with Jenny and her family. Sadly, her husband died and she had to close the shop. It is now a takeaway run by Mr Sam Yip and his wife.

Sam Yip outside his Chinese takeaway, Oriental House, 26 Aberllechau Road, circa 2000

No. 31   In the early days, this was a fish and chip shop but it became a draper's shop and boot maker's, owned by Mr & Mrs Thomas Wilcox, taken over later as a fish and chip shop by Richard Wilcox and May Simms. The business continued under Hilda Simms and, eventually, Glyn Powell.

No. 33   Mr Smith had a butcher's shop for a number of years. It was known as 'The Canadian Meat Supply Co' and was later taken over by Mr & Mrs Ebenezer Reynolds. Later still, it became a fish and chip shop when Mrs Haycock, who lived behind Jim the Butcher's shop, married Mr Taylor.

No. 34   John Davies's fish and chip shop – yet another one!

No. 35   This is 'Day's' shop, opened in 1912 by William Day. The family continued in business until 1983. During this time, it has seen so much of the village grow and change, the chapels once full, now empty; other shops come and go and the Butcher's Arms next door, burnt down, rebuilt and finally demolished. The National Colliery, which was so much a part of Wattstown, and which itself knew difficult times, closed in 1968. 'Days' has been in a position to see all these changes and Mrs Evelyn Maddern, nee Day, has survived the business and has such clear memories of people and events which have occurred during her lifetime. The shop was once a general store and barber shop, while upstairs, young men of the village met to put the world to right! They called it the 'Tupper Boys Club'. In 1983, Dennis and Kay Evans took over the shop with John, their son. Edwina Stuart, Rose Davies, Elaine Jones, and Anita Radcliffe are just a few of the local ladies who worked there.

Behind the Butcher's Arms, at the left hand side of 'The Arcade', stood a tin shed from which Mrs Rees 'Tallow' sold faggots and peas.

HILLSIDE TERRACE

No. 8   This was the front-room shop of 'Granny' Rachel Charles, in the 1920s. She sold sweets and general goods.

No. 24   Another front-room shop, of Mary Williams, general stores.

No. 37   Sam and Jane Morris kept this front-room shop as a general store until 1916.

No. 42   Robert Sampson, newsagents 1919.

No. 43   Mr & Mrs Glyn Griffiths had a fish and chip shop here. It was he who built 'Marks' - the tin shop in Pleasant View.

No. 50   Mrs Clissold had a sweet shop here, later taken over by Mrs Williams.

No. 63   This was Mr Knelms' the butcher's shop.

No. 70   Mr John Williams kept a shop here called 'Cash Stores'. It was later taken over by Ned Preece, who kept it as a grocery store.

No. 75   This was the draper's shop of Mrs Sarah Ann Jones in 1925, later taken over by William Bateman and eventually owned by Hugh Barrow.

No. 76   This was originally built to be a club, but the owners of the estate would not allow the sale of alcohol. In 1905, it was the shop and home of Mr Cardin who, being sympathetic to the cause of Bethel members, allowed them to meet in the warehouse under the shop. In 1916, Terry Stores took it over as a grocery shop, as part of the Thomas & Evans group of Porth. In 1972, it ceased to trade as Terry Stores, when Hugh Barrow took it over as a general stores. The shop, then, was run by a succession of owners, until the present owner, Parvitar Singh, who has occupied it since 1997.

No. 83   Mrs Williams' front room shop sold drapery and newspapers.

Mr Dan Phillips delivering the milk.

Mrs Jones the draper, of Hillside Terrace, circa 1930

P and M stores, once Terry Stores, part of the Thomas and Evans Group.

GLENSIDE PRINTING

Glenside, standing in its own grounds at the end of Hillside Terrace, was built in 1882-83 by the man who was responsible for sinking the shafts of the Cwtch Colliery.

Henry Lewis was a mining engineer and, with his partner Matthew Cope, leased the mineral rights of Aberllechau Farm in 1881. Until the houses of Hillside Terrace were built in 1884, the house stood alone, looking down on the colliery site.

Henry Lewis sold the colliery, and probably didn't spend much time at Glenside after the house was completed. It became the home of the colliery agent, and the first recorded resident was James Miles from Risca, where 'Watts Watts' already had a colliery at Wattsville. Over the years, the tenancy changed as the various colliery managers and agents were replaced.

The grounds were well laid out lawns at the front, and orchards at the rear, which were kept well tended by a number of gardeners and employees of the colliery.

It was always popular for choirs, football teams, etc, to have their photographs taken in front of the house, usually in the presence of the agent, sometimes even shaking hands. Many of the photographs in this book are evidence of this.

After the nationalisation of collieries in 1947, the house continued to be used, but when the pit closed in 1968, it lay empty and derelict. It was taken over by Mr. Glyn Davies, a printer from Penygraig. Over the last thirty-three years, the business has grown, and is recognised for the high quality work produced under the name of *Glenside Printing*.

CHAPEL STREET

The basement of Terry Stores first became home to the members of Bethel Free Mission, and later the Salvation Army held their Sunday School and services there under the leadership of Mr Chick.

In the 1920s, Victor Hudd opened a shoe repair business and later sold it to Arnold Lewis and George Thomas who, despite being deaf and dumb, knew which shoes belonged to which face. He continued with the business until the early 1950s.

No. 1   Thomas Morgan Jones's front-room shop in the 1920s.

Friends Vaughan Evans and Nicholas Herbert from the Cottage in Chapel Street.

BAILEY STREET

No. 33   Mrs Bounds' fish and chip shop - one more of the several in Wattstown over the years.

No. 81   'Strouds' the bakery. Mary Stroud began the business in the early 1900s. Later, William Stroud moved to 22 Lower Bailey Street.

VICTORIA TERRACE

No. 1   Dan Phillips had a dairy here for nearly 36 years, assisted after the Second World War by his eldest son, David.

No. 7   Mrs Tabitha Saunders' shop in 1915. Miss Saunders kept a sweet shop here in the 1940s, which some will remember as the place to buy sherbert and liquorice, and toffee dabs.

SCHOOL STREET

No. 21   Mrs Mahoney, who sold small beer.

No. 23   Mrs Willis's front-room shop sold home-made toffee.

No. 28   Mr Jones the milk - yet another dairy.

BRYN TERRACE

No. 7   Jones' front room shop during the 1920s.

No. 16   Mr Evans the dairy - later kept by Vaughan Evans, his son.

No. 18   Jane Davies' front-room shop.

PLEASANT VIEW

No. 17 For many years a fish and chip shop, run by Joyce Lloyd and then continued by Blod French, and eventually by Mary Thomas. It ceased to be a shop in the 1960s.

No. 18 This was also a fish and chip shop, run by Mr & Mrs William Evans – known as Lanky because the family came from Lancashire! It eventually became 'Enids', selling groceries, sweets, etc. It remained open all hours until her death in 1985.

No. 25 George Davies kept a shop here until the 1920s, when it was taken over by Bill Bateman, who kept it as a grocery store. Later, it was run by his children, Colin and Jean, with her husband George. It was sold to Rene and Neville Davies, who closed it as a shop in 1991.

No. 29 William Davies had a fish and chip shop here.

No. 44 This was the drapery shop of Mary Jones, sister to Sam Jones, overman in the National colliery. Mr & Mrs Trevor Collins live there now.

On the corner by the steps opposite No. 15, there were three shops at one time.

1. At the side of Marks' store, on the left, below the steps, was a butcher's shop owned by Evans the butcher, from Ynyshir. When this was demolished, the steps, which originally ran alongside the garden wall of 13 Bryn Terrace, were moved to their present position for easier access to the stores underneath Marks' shop.

Marks Shed, Pleasant View, circa 1930s.
Standing outside are: left to right, Rees Harris, George Thomas (deaf and dumb), Glyn Griffiths, Eben Thomas, Tom Griffiths, Mr Jones the postman.

*Enid Cull ('Lankey'), whose shop was literally 'open all hours'.
She had the nickname because her father came from Lancashire.*

*Neville and Rene Davies, at the doorway of their shop at No. 25 Pleasant View.
It was known for years as 'Batemans'. It closed in 1991.*

2.   'Marks' tin shed, where Mr Trevor Collins worked for 27 years, managing the shop for most of that time. The shop was originally built by Mr Tom Griffiths for his son Glyn and family of Hillside, and managed, prior to 1936, by Mr Frank Fishlock, of 22 Bryn Terrace. Many people from Wattstown have worked there, including Rene Bosley; Mary Seldon; Mary Atkins; Glenys Finnear; Anita Radcliffe; Eunice Hitchings. When Mr Marks closed it in 1963 it was taken over by various people including Mary Atkins, Ron Lusty, Tegwyn Davies, Ted Davies and eventually, Ken Harris.

Mr William James Marks had his business in Ynyshir, and Wattstown became his second shop. He had a son, Howard, and the shop became known as Howard's store. Mr W. J. Marks was an astute businessman and often advertised his wares in letters that Trevor Collins would have to push through people's letterboxes in his own time!

On the right side of Marks was another shop, which sold clothes, run by Mrs Blod Davies. This later became the sweet shop of Mr Palmer. There was at one time a cobblers here, with Mr Lewis and George Thomas, before they moved to Chapel Street, underneath Terry Stores.

'Pete ' the bread delivery man.

A PAGE FROM KELLY'S DIRECTORY OF BUSINESSES, 1900
WATTSTOWN 1901

Private Residents:

James Miles		Glenside
Rev. David Morris		68 Hillside Terrace

Commercial:

Benjamin Davies	*draper*	
George Davies	*boot warehouse*	
Morgan Davies	*hairdresser*	Aberllechau Road
Benjamin Jenkins	*hairdresser*	Aberllechau Road
Mrs Mary John	*shopkeeper*	Aberllechau Road
Thomas John		Wattstown Hotel
Henry M. Jones	*shopkeeper*	Post Office
Mrs Margaret Jones	*shopkeeper*	Aberllechau Road
David Lewis	*butcher*	Aberllechau Road
Mrs Mary Lewis		Butcher's Arms Public House
John Meredith	*fishmonger and fruiterer*	
James Miles	*colliery agent*	Glenside
William Morgan	*shopkeeper*	Aberllechau Road
Thomas Powell	*grocer*	Aberllechau Road
John Richards	*shopkeeper*	Hillside
Thomas Roberts	*shopkeeper*	
John Rowe	*butcher*	Aberllechau Road
United National Collieries Ltd.	'National Collieries'	
James Miles	*commercial agent*	
William Meredith	*manager*	
John Williams	*shopkeeper*	
Mrs Mary Williams	*newsagent & stationer*	Hillside
Mrs Mary Williams	*draper*	Hillside
R. Thomas Williams	*agent to Refuge Assurance Co.*	Hillside
William Williams	*shopkeeper*	Aberllechau Road

1906 KELLY'S TRADE DIRECTORY OF BUSINESSES

Samuel Cardin	*grocer (Terry Stores)*
William Day	
John Evans	*tailor*
Reynallt Ganter	*shopkeeper*
Walter Haggett	

Job Hoskins	*sub-postmaster*	
Thomas Jeffrey	*greengrocer*	
Ben Jenkins	*hairdresser*	
Miss Mary John	*shopkeeper*	
Thomas John	*Wattstown Hotel (Tommy Johns)*	
John Kane	*grocer*	
Mary Lewis	*Butcher's Arms*	
William Lewis	*shopkeeper*	
Thomas Powell	*Cambrian Stores*	
William Reed	*butcher*	
John Rees	*shopkeeper*	
Ann Richards	*shopkeeper*	
John Rowe	*butcher*	
Mary Stroud	*bakers*	
Walter T. Griffiths	*agent*	
John Williams	*shopkeeper*	

1920 KELLY'S TRADE DIRECTORY

The Canadian Meat Supply Co.	*butcher*	33 Aberllechau Road
George Davies	*shopkeeper*	25 Pleasant View
John Davies	*fried fish*	34 Aberllechau Road
Thomas John Davies	*doctor*	25 Aberllechau Road
William Day		35 Aberllechau Road
William Evans		18 Pleasant View
Annie Haycock	*butcher*	9 Aberllechau Road
George Hill		Wattstown Hotel
Evan Jones		
Mary Jones		
Irene Meredith		20 Aberllechau Road
Sarah Maud Mills		27 Pleasant View
Charles Thomas	*dairy*	
Thomas Powell		8 Aberllechau Road
Evan Rees	*boot repairs*	9a Aberllechau Road
Ebenezer Reynolds	*butcher*	33 Aberllechau Road
Robert Sampson	*newsagent*	42 Hillside Terrace
Mrs Tabitha Saunders		7 Victoria Terrace
Thomas & Evans		76 Hillside Terrace
Morgan J. Roberts	*Secretary of Institute*	
W. John Wells	*fried fish*	22 Aberllechau Road
Thomas Wilcox	*draper & boot maker*	31 Aberllechau Road

Workmen's Institute

Pensioners, on a trip to the coast, waiting for the bus outside the Institute

In the early years of the 20th century, the centres of social and cultural life in Wattstown were the chapels and the public houses. These were the only public buildings available.

In 1909, a committee of men were given the task of building an institute for the benefit of the working men of Wattstown, together with rooms for entertainment for the people of the village. It was to include a gymnasium for the use of young people, both employed and unemployed, in need of physical recreation.

The committee were known as the Executive Council of the Wattstown Workmen's Institute, and these are their names:

Frank Harwood, J. M. Vaughan, S. G. Clissold, J. Nicholas, William Price, Samuel Mason, E. G. Cross, George Evans, John Harris, George Thomas, John Hyer, W. H. Jones, Evan David Evans, Thomas David Evans

The witness to this contract was George E. Watts, of 1 Lower Bailey Street.

The building was begun on 13th September, 1909 and completed by 9th April 1910, at a cost of £2,747. The cost was borne by the National Colliery Company. The builders were Messrs Evans Bros., Woodville Road, Cardiff, and the architect was B. Huxham, 22 Graig Road, Ynyshir. The ground was purchased from the Bailey Estates Trustees.

The Institute brought a new dimension to the village, with a library, reading room, concert hall, games room and its gymnasium - complete with 'ropes'!

The Institute quickly became a popular centre of social activity and it was widely used. During times of hardship in the long strikes and lock-outs of 1912, 1921 and 1926, it became a centre for soup kitchens and was used by the unemployed to pass away the long hours of inactivity. The concert hall, with its stage and balcony was a popular venue for concerts, choirs and other artistes. It was the centre for prize-giving and awards for all the activities of the clubs that met there. Cantatas, dramas and charity concerts to raise money for local causes meant that it was a busy place.

The Institute opened its doors to the early members of Bethel, who held their Sunday School Anniversaries and sisterhood meetings there, until they found their own premises in School Street.

The gymnasium was well used and, in 1928, the newly formed Boys' Club made use of the facilities, until they moved into their own new clubhouse in 1932.

An active committee ran the Institute. Frank Harwood was vice-chairman, and later chairman, a position he held for 25 years until 1934. M. J. Roberts became the new chairman until 1937, and was followed by Ivor Thomas. The caretaker for many years was Tom Thomas. Many a bus trip began outside the main entrance, travelling to all parts of Wales.

The committee consisted of miners and colliery officials, while the chairman was the colliery manager, and his secretary became the committee secretary. Each District in the pit had its own teams — bowls, billiards, darts, skittles and racing pigeons, and there was much competition between them.

167

Inside the Institute, on the occasion of a meal and presentation to Dr and Mrs Ernest Orr, circa 1930.

The Wattstown Workmen's Institute billiards teams, the Burroughs & Watts Shield winner, circa 1935.

The Institute was home to these teams who met at various times, while their annual prize presentation evening was a big event. In 1959, Wattstown Colliery Tote was formed and the committee felt the Institute should become a Social Club, with the sale of alcohol. This began later in the year with the assistance of the Fernvale Brewery Company.

The committee consisted of the following:

Secretary	Tom Kenealy
Chairman	Idris Griffiths
Treasurer	Glyn Powell
Trustees	Eddie Reeves, Richard Prangley, Alf King, Albert Down, Trevor Gwilym, Billy Woods.

The tote was able to offer prizes of £100, £75, £50, and £25, which was a respectable sum in those days. Mr Jack Lloyd became tote treasurer and remained so until the pit closed in 1968. The Institute was maintained by the contributions of the miners, deducted from their wages. The demise of the colliery saw the end of the Institute as a social centre and the building was sold to the Rhondda Borough Council, after lying empty for a number of years. The building was used as a Senior Citizens' Centre, providing lunches and various activities for the people of the community. The Centre ceased to be used for meals in 2000, as the Rhondda Cynon Taff council sought to cut costs. The building by then had deteriorated and the upper floor could no longer be used. Sadly, it is no longer the busy, well-used place it once was and the years have added to its problems for, like the chapels and the church, people find their interests and enthusiasm in other directions. The building that was once the social centre of the community waits for another generation to revive it.

Wattstown Institute Committee's Visit to St. Athan's Camp.

THE Wattstown Institute Committee formed a party of about thirty, and took their annual trip to the St. Athan's Camp, on Saturday afternoon, June 5th. The journey down developed the usual alarming appetites, and the whole party did full justice to the

The party split into small groups, each seeking its pleasure, according to its own interest. Some made for the swimming pool, others went for a walk along the sea shore and on the adjoining Leys Golf Course, whilst the more energetic joined the boys in cricket, and, on such a day, even football!

comestible abundance put before them on their arrival.

Rain clouds at Wattstown were left behind, and blue sky and fierce sun prevailed at St. Athan, and the Camp certainly looked its best.

Towards ten o'clock, the crowd, very tired and very happy, returned by twos and threes to the Camp, and added to the cheerful and noisy sing-songsters in the Concert Hall, where a pleasant half-hour was spent before the bus was boarded for home.

The Wattstown Workmen's Institute

Winners of the Summer Snooker League and finalists of the NCB Billards Competition 1960

Back row (left to right): Iorrie Leavis, R. Norris, A. Uzzell (chairman), W. King, W. Kenealy (Sec), D. Roberts, B. Davies, R. Hughes

Front row: J. Evans, J. Lloyd (vice captain), B. Wakeford, T. Thomas (captain), A Kemp, A. Jones, C. Anstey

Back row (left to right): Dennis Evans (secretary), R. Hughes, K. Harris, L. Butcher, T. Thomas, A. Uzzell (chairman)
Front row: G. Martin, Johnny Downes, E Ocvain (captain), W. Hughes (vice captain), Neville Davies, M. Martin

Wattstown Memorial Park

Photograph of Wattstown Memorial Park when it was first opened in 1922.

© Wattstown Memorial Park

The Wattstown Memorial Park was opened in 1922 at a cost of £10,000, paid for by the United National Colliery Company. The work of draining, clearing and levelling the site was done by volunteers - mainly the local miners. Mr Smout was the first park-keeper, and it became a welcome amenity. Carnivals and gymkhanas were held on the football field and were very popular in the 1920s, during times of unemployment and depression. Robert Clarke organized motor cycle trials and competitions there, and the Park was well used for other events, as well as the usual soccer and rugby games.

The swimming baths were very popular with the young people and visitors came from far and wide to leap into the waters of Wattstown baths! The cold water came piped down from the colliery feeder – (brrr!), while some warmer water was introduced from the steam condenser in the colliery.

There was a slimy bottom to the pool and the water would become very murky. No filtration plants in those days! The young people would help to clean it on Saturdays. Costumes could be purchased from the pay offices and everyone thoroughly enjoyed themselves!

The park boasted tennis courts and an active tennis club which included: Eurfron Griffiths, Gwenda Davies, Jack Evans, Morlais Jones, Lily Holland, Reg Holland and David Daniels (secretary), Cyril Gilbert, Gronow Pugh, Linda Parr and many others.

The busy swimming baths in the Park, circa 1920s

Wattstown Amateur Football Club, 1919-1920.

Back row (left to right): George Thomas, ?, George Perrott, ?, Ted Crew.

3rd row: George Thompson, Tom Thomas, Will Southern, Tom Wilmore, David Bird, Neil Priest, Fred Martin, Ed Llewelyn, ? Hicks, ? Phillips, David Stevens.

2nd row: Dr Hughes, Reg Gunter, Ted Minty, Tom Evans, Stan Stroud, John Thomas, John Kane M.E.

Front row: Ivor Parry, Chris Wiltshire, Isaac Rees.

Wattstown Cricket Club, 1927.
Back row (left to right): David Daniels, Reg Holland, Bill Baker,
Middle row: Ernest Edwards, Jack Jones, Robert Edwards, Amos Griffiths
Front row: Thomas Dodd, Morgan Rees, Robert Jenkins, Jim Phelps, Alf Wilshire.

There were bowling greens, too, and Wattstown Bowling Club contained many good players, some of whom represented Wales at international matches and at the Empire Games. The Pavilion Buffet was a shop which sold sweets and cigarettes, and hot and cold drinks. A playground for children, with a paddling pool and shelter, was built in 1936, again with the help of volunteers. This was opened by Captain Geoffrey Crawshay in July of that year.

Both the Park and the Workmen's Institute were maintained by the National Colliery workers paying 3d. a week. Unfortunately, rising costs meant that they could no longer maintain both, and it was decided by the Workmen's Institute Committee to concentrate their efforts on keeping the Institute open. The Park became financially unsupported and closed its gates for two years. Mr Alfie Trow, the groundsman, had lived in the Park house since 1939, and he continued to maintain the Park during those two years, mowing the greens and cutting the hedges. When the Rhondda Urban District Council eventually took over responsibility for the Park, it was in good condition.

Soon after this, in 1959, the memorial gates were removed — apparently for repair, but they were never seen again and it remains a mystery to this day as to where they actually went! The new gates that now swing on the old pillars are not a patch on the originals, which were erected as a memorial to those who had died in the 'Great War'.

Wattstown en Fête

Opening of the Memorial Park

The opening of the Wattstown Memorial Park on Tuesday, 11th April, 1922 by
Sir Shadforth Watts, President of Watts Watts and the United National Collieries Ltd

Tuesday was a red-letter day in the annals of Wattstown, on the occasion of the formal opening of the Wattstown Memorial Park. There was a large number of distinguished visitors and the opening ceremony was performed by Sir F. Shadforth Watts, chairman of the United National Collieries Ltd. Prior to the opening ceremony, a luncheon was held in a marquee adjacent to the Park, when Sir Shadforth Watts presided.

Amongst those present were:

Sir F. Shadforth Watts and Mrs Hugh Watts; the Right Hon. W. C. Bridgeman M.P. (Secretary of the Mines Department); Col Wylie; Col Curre C.B.E. and Mrs Curre; Major E. M. Watts M.C.; the Hon Akers Douglas; Lieut Edmund Watts R.N.; Sir Walter P. Nicholas; Lieut Col D. Watts Morgan; D.S.O. M.P.; Mr Will John M.P.; Mr D. Lleufer Thomas (the Rhondda Stipendiary); Councillor John Kane M.E. (General Manager of the United National Collieries); D. William Jenkins M.O.H; Councillor W. P. Thomas; Miss Williams; Messrs Edward Edwards; P. O. Ward; John Duncan; Dyer Lewis; John Kane; S. K. George; F. M. Eaton Fearn; James Miles; Mrs Becker; Mrs F. S. Carlton; Messrs Beresford; R. Heaton; Hedley Clarke (General Manager of the Cambrian Combine Collieries); F. J. Humphries; W. T. Griffiths; W. D. Rees; Ernest D. Williams; Dr D. H. Davies; Dr T. J. Davies; Dr Man Martin; Rev H. J. Davies; Messrs E. Arnott; Idris Price; R. W. McKenzie; Alfred Topal; W. P. Edwards; E. A. H. Benson; Dan Phillips; G. H. Platt; S. O. Clissold; Evan Thomas; B. H. Huxham; Arthur Williams; P. R. O. Hughes; William James; John Bell; Mrs F. J. Humphreys; Miss R. Griffiths; Mrs J. G. Francis; Councillor John Hughes; Dr M. C. Hurley; Mrs William James; Miss Miles; Mrs S. C. Richards; Mrs Dyer Lewis; Miss Richards; Miss M.Thomas; Mrs A. T. James; Mrs John Peel; Rev J. Wilson Roberts; Major Trevor Brecker; Capt A. T. James; Rev T. Evan Davies; Rev J. Pierce Price; Rev. E. C. Davies; Councillor W. J. Benjamin; Dr Price Evans; Deputy Chief Constable J. Williams; Inspector Thomas; Inspector Griffiths; Messrs William Price; G. J. Parry; B. E. Blackledge; J. S.Vincent; H. Morgan; H. A. Davies; Joseph Jenkins; David Thomas (British Legion); Robert Jones; J. F. Gregory; R. Yorath; J. G. Francis; Ronald George; S. C. Richards; G. T. Causton; J. Thomas; P. G. Smith (agent of Crawshay Bailey Estate); H. S. Watts; E D. James; E. T. Harcombe; Evan Richards; E. J. Reeves; J. R. Owen; Edgar Lewis; George Thomas; Rees Quilford; Thomas Vivian; Mark Stevens; William Jenkins; James Nicholas; C. R. Dickson; Stanley Winmill; W. T. Parry; John Jones; David Jenkins; Lewis Rhys; Rhys Dodd; William Price; Frank Harwood; Tom Bowen; Matt Jones; M. J. Roberts; Thomas Maundrell; Thomas Rees; Evan Parry; David Thomas; A. Glyndwr Thomas; James Rosser; George Hopkins; T. G. Moore; Daniel James; T. J. T. Thomas; George Evans; Samuel Mason; David Gough; David J. Rees and Thomas Thomas.

After the loyal toast had been proposed by the Chairman, the Right Hon W. C. Bridgeman proposed 'The Wattstown Memorial and Recreation Park'. He said that when he accepted the invitation to attend that function, the Geddes axe was hanging over their heads and he was not sure in what capacity he would be able to appear.

He did not know whether it would be as Secretary for Mines or as an ex-Secretary. He was pleased to say that the Mines Department remained whole.

On behalf of the Mines Department, he said he wished to congratulate those who had brought about this Recreation Park. Recreation, such as the Wattstown community would now be able to indulge in, would help to bring the people together more, and help them to understand each other better: it would also be a great boon in the way of health.

He would like to see similar things done in every colliery district throughout the country.

The members of the National Park committee and their chairman, Mr John Kane, must have worked very hard and shown a great deal of perseverance and patience to bring the work to such a successful finish. He asked leave to couple with the toast the name of Mr John Kane.

Mr Kane, in rising to reply, was heartily applauded. He spoke of the state of affairs regarding recreation twenty years ago. At that time, he said, Wattstown had no lights and no roads. In fact, they had 'no nothing', (laughter). They had both a cricket and a football team and he was captain of both. Their greatest enemy, at that time, was the river, which was continually claiming their ground. From time to time, raids had to be made and the river dammed back, even if it had to be diverted on to someone else's property.

It was ten years ago when they opened their Institute and provided the community with indoor recreation. The Institute provided for billiards, reading, gymnastics and other indoor pastimes. In all these efforts, he had to mention the Crawshay Bailey Estate, who had always been staunch friends. When the Institute was opened, they came forward with great financial assistance. On the present occasion, they had given six acres of land practically free. The committee, Mr Kane said, also had a benevolent fund which provided every old man, widow and sick person in the village with a present every Christmas.

In instances where poor people had experienced bad luck, they were helped with monetary grants. They also had a nursing association which helped in cases of sickness or accident. In addition to all these, they had the colliery band, which won the Welsh Championship Competition two years in succession, and the Wattstown Royal Male Voice Choir, the quality of which they would have an opportunity of judging for themselves that afternoon. The question was often asked, 'Did efforts of this kind pay?' He said emphatically, both from the point of view of a social worker and a materialistic employer of labour, 'Yes'. During the last six or seven years, the colliery had experienced a very trying time. A large number of strikes had taken place – some general and some local. During the whole of that period, they did not experience one moment of anxiety. Collieries on all sides of them were stopped, but their colliery was not. During the five years of war, the colliery worked 1509 days, averaging 302 days per year. There was a general stoppage in 1915, when they lost three days, and in 1916 there were fifty-three Sundays and one blizzard (laughter). He doubted if there was any other colliery in the country that could equal them. The Park which they were opening that day was a memorial to the men who went to the war, but it was also a memorial to the men who stayed at home. They had representatives of the colliery men there, also representatives from their other collieries and he thought that it ought to be put on record that, during all those trying years, those men never overlooked their duty to the men who were at the Front (applause).

'The United National Collieries Ltd.' was proposed by Mr B. R. Heaton, who said that during the thirty years that he had been associated with the Crawshay Bailey Estate, he could not think of a single occasion on which there has been friction between them and the colliery company.

He was not sure that he ought not to retire, so that the spell might not be broken. (*laughter*). He could not imagine a more fitting memorial than the Park which they were shortly going to open. For generations to come, it would, undoubtedly, provide pleasure to residents of Wattstown. He could not help recalling the opening of the Institute, which took place twelve years ago, and seeing with pleasure that many who were gathered together at that ceremony were also there that day.

Sir Shadforth Watts, who was greeted with hearty applause, responded. He expressed his gratitude to the Crawshay Bailey Estate and to Colonel and Mrs Curre for the great help that they had given to the movement. He thanked them all heartily on behalf of the company, for the way in which they had received the toast.

'Our Guests' was proposed by Mr James Miles, who said that if all the mineral lessors in South Wales had realised their obligations to the same extent as the Crawshay Bailey Estate, there would not have been such prejudice against mineral lessors as was shown during the sitting of the Sankey Commission. Whenever they had approached the trustees, they had never come away empty-handed. The trustees helped considerably on the occasion of the Institute, and they had also been great helpers with regard to the present occasion, and he felt sure that the same thing would happen the next time they asked (*laughter and applause*). He felt sure they all very much regretted the absence of Mabon and sincerely hoped that he would soon be restored to good health again. Colonel Curre, in replying, said 'United' was the name of the colliery and he thought it was a suitable name. They had taken for their motto, 'Live and Let Live'. Mr Kane said he might some day want more help. If what he wanted was in aid of such a good cause, he (the speaker) felt sure he would get it.

Sir Walter Nicholas also responded.

Lieut-Col D. Watts Morgan proposed 'The Chairman' and said that Sir Shadforth was a man of few words but great deeds. His name was well known in connection with coal and shipping all over the world. During the time that he (Colonel Watts Morgan) was at Wattstown, they did not have a single stoppage. He sincerely hoped that the employer and the workmen, especially the latter, would return to sanity and sit around the table and hammer out their differences as they used to do. It was only in that way that they could keep the wheels turning (*applause*).

Sir Shadforth Watts responded.

During the luncheon, selections were given by the Ynyshir & Wattstown Silver Band and by the Royal Wattstown Male Voice Choir. After the luncheon, Sir Shadforth Watts formally opened the grounds and addresses were given by Mr W. C. Bridgeman, M.P., Mr D. Lleufer Thomas and Mr William John, M.P. The Park, situated close to the Wattstown colliery, comprises six acres of land. It includes football and cricket fields, bowling green, children's playground, terrace walks, swimming bath and tennis courts. It is proposed to add a bandstand and also dressing rooms for the footballers, towards which £1200 has been paid into the welfare fund by the company. The catering was ably carried out by Messrs Stevens (Confectioners) Ltd., French Confectioners, Dorothy and Dutch Cafes, Cardiff.

(courtesy of The South Wales News)

Fancy Dress at the Wattstown Carnival, during the 1926 Strike

Carnival, Sports and Baby Shows

A successful carnival was held at the Wattstown Memorial Park on Thursday of last week in aid of the local Workmen's Benevolent Fund. There were numerous entries, and the procession attracted the attention of the whole district. Mr John Kane, M.E., General Manager of the United National Collieries distributed the prizes.

The officials were: Secretary - Mr J. Roberts; Judges - Mrs Hugh Watts, Mrs John Kane, Messrs Daniel Phillips and T. J. Thomas (Carnival Characters); Mr W. D. Rees, M.R.C.V.S. (Horses); Lieut-Colonel D. Watts Morgan, C.B.E. D.S.O., M.P., and Lieut. E. H. Watts R.N. (Ambulance Squads, Boy Scouts, etc).

CARNIVAL

The following were the awards:

Best Character (lady or gent):	Miss Florrie Stevens, *'Roundabout'*
Best-dressed Cyclist and Cycle:	Merlin Langford
Best Comic Character:	H. Evans Treherbert, *'Zulu Chief'*
Best Fancy Dress:	Miss Annie Evans, *'Cinderella'*
Special:	Miss Phyllis Mills, *'Bathing Girl'*
Best Fancy Dress (mounted):	D. S. Lewis, Porth, *'Crusader'*
Special:	Victor Jones, *'Red Indian'*
Best Historical Character:	Theo Phillips, *'Sir Walter Raleigh'*
Best Character (boy, under 14)	Wattstown School:

1. Alfie Trow, *'Rag and Bone Merchant'*
2. Edwin Lye, *'Zulu'*
3. Thomas Richards, *'Balkan Shepherd'*

Best Character (girl, under 14) Wattstown School:

1. Meriel Hughes, *'Superstition'*
2. Catherine Stone, *'Bubbles'*
3. Gladys Evans, *'Dick Whittington'*

Best Character (infants)

1. Enid and Alma Bird, *'Darby and Joan'*
2. John and Leslie Owen, *Jimmy Wilde and Pete Herman'*
3. Emlyn Jenkins, *'Lloyd George'*

Best Character (boy, under 14) Open: Walter Foxwell, *'Donaghue'*.

Best Character (girl, under 14) Open: Agnes Rees.

Fancy Dress at the Wattstown Carnival during the 1926 Strike

Clowns in the Carnival in the Park during the 1926 Strike

Fancy Dress outside Wattstown Park, 1926.
Miss Sally Thompson, who later married Hugh Jones 'Patch' of Pleasant View, with a friend.

Best Tableau (not less than six):	United National Office Staff (Dickens characters).
Best Tradesman's Turnout:	J. R. Thomas, Porth.
Best Colliery Horse:	Jones and Jones, Abergorky.
Best Cart Horse:	George Masters, Porth.
Best Jazz Band:	Jack Evans (Wattstown Band).
	Mrs Mills (Female Band).
Special:	Leonard Willis (School Street Band).
Group of 10 or 12 with officer:	Wattstown Boy Scouts (Scoutmaster, C Noot)
Best Ambulance Squad :	1, Ynyshir; 2, Ferndale No 3.
Best Cadet on route:	Scout Keneally.

A young group of St John Ambulance, after winning the Cup and a Rose Bowl in the Wattstown Carnival in the Park in 1930.
Included in the photograph are; Eddie Rees, Ken Rowney, G Rowney, Ken Dale, Tom Davies, D. Jones, Phil Dixon, Tom Rees,
E. Griffiths, Glyn Evans, C. Grundy.

BABY SHOW WINNERS

The Baby Show, which was held on the same afternoon, needless to say attracted many entries and, judging from the number of exhibits, particularly bonny babies appear to bloom in Wattstown. Dr C. Maclellan and Dr Mackenzie were the judges, assisted by District Nurse Davies and Nurses Edwards, Bond and Israel (of the Rhondda Urban District Council nursing staff).

The chief awards were as follows :

Class 1 (six months and under):
1. David William Foster; 2. Elunud M. Thomas; 3. Raymond J. Lewis.

Class 2 (twelve months and under):
1. Emlyn Hawkins; 2. Olive Bailey; 3. Glyn Roberts.

Class 3 (eighteen months and under):
1. Winifred Raikes; 2. Ieuan Evans; 3. Noel Featherstone.

Class 4 (two years and under):
1. Iris E. Morris; 2. William G. Richardson; 3. Robert Weightman.

Class 5 (twins two years and under):
1. Blodwen Thomas and Marion B Thomas.
2. Douglas N. Cross and Dorane J. Cross;
3. Leslie Evans and Haydn H. Evans;

Class 6 (best babies fed on cows' milk):
1. William Edward Williams (Jones Milk Vendor, Ynyshir)

 Altogether, over 130 babies were examined.

Baby Show at the Wattstown Baths, 1928

Wattstown Amateur Football Club, Cup winners 1947-48.

Back row (left to right): Dewi Davies, —?, Len Bateman, Mr Bundy (Colliery Manager,) Cyril Greedy, Alf Phelps, Charlie Little, Bill Bateman.

Middle row: Idwal Roberts, (Butchers Arms), Vince Edwards, Dick Marney, Dick Morris, Jones Franklin, Eben Davies, Bill Ward, Idris Griffiths, Albert Uzzell.(senior)

Front row: Les Owen, Marsden Davies, Len Lewis, Garfield Winter (captain), Jim French, Bill Cameron, Jim Little.

Front: Albert Uzzell, Clive Hedditch.

SPORTS

The results were as follows:

100 Yards Handicap (Open):
1, Ivor Day, Wattstown: 2, E J Thomas, Wattstown.

300 Yards Handicap (Open):
1, Emrys Davies, Tylorstown; 2, H. James, Pontygwaith.

100 Yards Handicap (confined to workmen and Institute members):
1, Garfield Silcox, Ynyshir; 2, Thomas Evans, Wattstown.

100 Yards Handicap:
(confined to workmen and Institute members, fourteen to sixteen years of age);
1, W. J. Davies, Wattstown; 2, Glyn Phillips, Wattstown.

100 Yards Ex-Servicemen (confined to members of British Legion Ynyshir):
1, H. Minnett ,Ynyshir; 2, Isaac Rees, Wattstown.

100 Yards Ex- Servicemen (Open):
1, W. J. Lewis, Porth.

100 Yards Obstacle Race (Confined):
1, Ivor Stephens, Wattstown. 2, Ivor Day, Wattstown.

100 Yards Hurdle Race (Confined):
1, Sam Baker, Ynyshir ; 2, W. H. Lloyd, Wattstown.

80 Yards Girls Race:
1, Enid Bird, Wattstown; 2, Doris Davies, Ynyshir.

Tilting the Basket:
1, Ivor Day and Ivor Stephens; 2, Joseph Eland and partner.

Ambulance Competition:
1, Ynyshir (captain, Sam Atkins).

Nursing Competition: 1, Ynyshir (captain Mrs Chapman).

Individual Ambulance Competition:
1, William Davies, Ynyshir.

100 Yards Wattstown Schoolboys:
1, Walter Smith, Wattstown; 2, James Kane, Wattstown.

100 Yards Ynyshir Schoolboys:
1, Willie Phillips, Ynyshir; 2, Cyril Rowlands, Ynyshir.

100 Yards Challenge Cup Race:
1, Ivor Powell, Ynyshir Schools.

The Coal Beauty Queen 1963, taken in the Park. Included in the photograph are Albert Down, Vic Locke, Alan Jones (Undermanager), Albert Uzzell.

The Memorial Park Gates today — not the original ones.

Wattstown Bowls Club

Wattstown Bowls Club, circa 1922

Back row (left to right): Isaac Rees, Tom Evans, Ivor Stephens, D. Morley, D. J. Stevens, George Thompson, J. H. Owen, George Evans.
3rd row: Mark Stevens, John Cross, Ernest Holland, Bill Reeves, R. Fisher, Sergeant Moore (policeman), Tom Thomas, Evan Evans,
David Jones, Dr J. J. Hughes.
2nd row: George Thomas, J. Kane, Will John Stevens, W. J. Griffiths, John Kane M.E., J. Jenkins, Jim Rosser, Albert Fisher, Onslow Reagan.
In front: David Jones, A. Fisher

A number of Rhondda club representatives met in March 1914 and formed the "Rhondda Valleys Bowling League". Wattstown at that time had no facilities for Bowls, and it wasn`t until the opening of Wattstown Memorial Park in 1921 that greens became available, laid under the auspices of the Miners' Welfare Association, and financed by the Miners' Welfare Fund.

Wattstown were admitted to the League in 1922, and that year won the team competition in Division 1, for the first time. They repeated this achievement again in 1982. Over the years, Wattstown bowlers have acquitted themselves well and have a record to be proud of. The South African Bowls Team paid a visit to Britain in 1932, and included in their tour, playing Wattstown in the Memorial Park.

There are so many that have maintained the high standards that Welsh bowling has come to represent, but here are some of the names recorded in the Official Records.

Welsh Bowls Association:

R. Mays and I. Mays, runners-up, Pairs Competition, 1976.

P. Turton, D. Maundrell, C. Diamond, runners-up, Triples Competition, 1982.

P. Turton, D. Maundrell, C. Diamond, winners, Triples Competition, 1983.

R. Williams, W. G. Kent, M. Manweiller, I. Rees, winners, Rinks Competition, 1934.

Mid Glamorgan Bowling Associations:

R. Mays and K. Gilder, runners-up, Pairs Competition, 1976.

D. Maundrell, G. Wilshire, P. Turton, winners, Triple Competition, 1974.

D. Maundrell, P. Turton, C. Diamond, winners, Triple Competition, 1982.

P. Turton, L . Davies, D. Maundrell, C. Diamond, runners-up, Rink Competition, 1985

D. Foulkes, K. Cronin, G. Jones, G. Gilder, runners-up, Rinks Competition, 1986.

D. Foulkes, K. Cronin, G. Jones, G. Gilder, winners, Rinks Competition, 1987.

A. G. H. Wilshire   League Chairman, 1968.

R. Mays   League Chairman, 1979.

E. G. Owen   League Chairman, 1986.

R. Mays   Tournament Secretary, 1976-77.

R. Mays   League Secretary, 1981-.

Among the Rhondda bowlers who have represented Wales at the Commonwealth Games was Spencer Wilshire, the son of Caleb Wilshire of Bailey Street. He has achieved many trophies including the British Isles Pairs Championships in 1976, 1979 and 1981, in partnership with Lyn Perkins, both of the Tonypandy Club.

The visit of the South African Bowls Team to Wattstown in 1932

The Wattstown Bowls Club in the Park, 1934

BOWLS
WATTSTOWN v TROEDYRHIW.

at Wattstown Park (W.B.A.) on Saturday.

Scores:
WATTSTOWN

Rink 1:

D. Pugh, Jack John, Herb Davies, and Ivor Parmee (skip) 18

Rink 2:

D. Rowlands, W. Lloyd, George Cross, and Ben Davies (skip) 24

Rink 3:

 P. Morgans, W. Bound, R. Jarman, and J. Jenkins (skip) 26

Rink 4:

R . Stroud, T. J. Thomas, E. J. Evans, and Ike Rees (skip) 18

Total 86

TROEDYRHIW

Rink 1:

J. Hughes, E. Williams, Ed Evans, and L . Pugh (skip) 15

Rink 2:

E. J. Jones, D. J. Thomas, C. Tovey, and W. C. Morgan (skip) 18

Rink 3:

T. Evans, T. R. Jones, W. Gameyham, and R. Yeo (skip) 16

Rink 4:

B. Evans, Syd Tovey, J. E. Jones, and D. Morton (skip) 18

Total 67

Wattstown won by 19 shots.

Allotments

Wattstown Gardeners Society Shed.
Left to right: Messrs Jack Collins, Trevor Collins, and Byron Seldon.

The Wattstown Gardeners Allotment Society c.2000.
Left to right: David Ward, Ken Evans, Edgar Evans, Byron Seldon, Brian Wadforth, Trevor Collins,
Hugh Barrow, Jack Collins, Douglas Davies.

Wattstown, Bird's Eye View.

This photograph was taken in approximately 1932. Note how neat and tidy everything looks. The plots below the farm road were offered to the unemployed miners of Wattstown by the Crawshay Bailey estate in 1926. This was the year of a seven-month strike and the plots, known as 'quarter acres' were offered to anyone who was prepared to cultivate them. This was a difficult time for many, with a shortage of money and food. Among those who took up the offer were:

Mr Beal, Hillside Terrace; Mr Robert Jenkins, Chapel Street; Mr Tom Hughes, Chapel Street; Mr Jack Collins, School Street; Mr Fred Martin, Hillside Terrace; Mr Evan Jones, Bryn Terrace; Mr Cottrell, Heol Llechau; Mr Alf Green, School Street; Mr Hitchins, Heol Llechau; Mr Trow, Pleasant View; Mr and Mrs Davies, Pleasant View and Mr and Mrs Jones (Painter), of School Street, kept pigs on the plots just below the farm road.

It is sad to see the area now derelict and overgrown, no longer required in these more affluent times.

Above the farm road can be seen the present-day allotments.

Jack Collins, Cefn Road with a Certificate of Merit awarded for one of his many achievements as a gardener

The Wattstown and District Allotment Association began on 11th April 1931, when an agreement was signed between the Crawshay Bailey estate and the Allotment Trustees, consisting of:

Edward James Reeves, Bryngarw, Elias Ralph, 35 Bailey Street and Joseph Henry Warren Morgan, 24 Bryn Terrace. The ground consisted of 10 plots of 10 perches area, at a ground rent of 1 shilling per annum (5p)

Those who were members of the Association at the start were as follows:

Plot Holders :

William Hawkins, Thomas Addis, H. L. Ballinger, F. R. Morris, Wyndham King, Joseph E. Hitchings, Lewis Enoch, Albert Uzzell, J. H. T. Smith, Cifford Gully, David Jones, Edward Lye.

The Association continues to this day, with many members making use of the excellent facilities for buying gardening products. Over the 70 years since its formation, many of its members have produced gardens of the highest quality. We have to congratulate those who, over the years, have consistently won prizes in competitions.

In one year, Wattstown was proud to see three men winning 1st. Prize for flowers, 1st. Prize for vegetables, and 1st. Prize for flowers and vegetables mixed. They were, of course, Ivor Rosser, Jack Lloyd, and Jack Collins.

They have won many trophies for their gardens and represent the finest among the gardeners of Wattstown.

204

Wattstown Boys Club

October 1928 saw the official formation of the Wattstown Boys Club, with a membership of 200 boys aged from 12 to 21 years. This had been in the planning stage for a while and met in the Workmen's Institute, not having a club building of their own. Gymnastic classes were first to begin on October 23rd, 1928, under the leadership of Tom Lister, with 135 boys present.

The Secretary of the Club was George Higgs and the Club was organised under the South Wales Miners' Boys Club Federation. This organisation was encouraged and supported by the Miners' Welfare and the Ocean Coal Company.

The Club was divided into the following branches, with section leaders at that time being:

1.	Dramatics	Owen Morris
2.	Ambulance	Ken Maundrell
3.	Table Tennis	William Barrow
4.	Netball	Robert Jenkins
5.	Physical Training	Charles Mason
6.	Indoor Games	Clifford Baistow
7.	Draughts	Edward Kennealy
8.	Hobbies	Simon Jones
9.	Association Football	Timothy Kane
10.	Rugby	H. Matthews
11.	Billiards	David Smith
12.	Cross Country	Idris Evans

The Club continued to use the Institute for its indoor activities and many attended the St. Athan Boys' Camp, which was organised, together with the use of playing fields and other boys' clubs, under the South Wales Miners' Welfare Fund. It wasn't until 1932 that a clubhouse was finally built. It was erected on ground situated at the river's edge, where the builders' merchants now stand.

It was designed by W. D. Morgan, architect, and built by Charles Jenkins, builders, of Porth, at a cost of £2500. It contained a main hall to seat 350 people, together with facilities for billiards, games, hobbies, a library, a buffet and offices. On 24th September 1932, it was officially opened by the Earl of Plymouth. It was the first building set up by the South Wales Federation of Boys' Clubs led by Captain J. Glynn-Jones.

Lord Davies of Llandinam, founder of the Ocean Coal Company, was one of the few mineowners who took an interest in the welfare of his workers and their communities. He strongly supported the Miners' Welfare Fund, and the South Wales Federation of Boys' Club.

The young people were encouraged to take advantage of the facilities of the Club and also to attend the St.Athan Boys' Camp. Both were intended to build character and offered sport and recreation.

Many will have fond memories of these visits to camp, at a time when holidays away were very rare, unless you were lucky enough to have a relative somewhere with whom you could stay!

There's no doubting the good influence that the Club had on those who were part of it, with its varied activities and the dedicated leaders who gave freely of their time and efforts to ensure its success.

Among these was the Institute Committee Secretary, Morgan J. Roberts, a well-respected man who had worked hard towards the building of the new club premises. The Club Treasurer was Robert Jenkins of Chapel Street and the first caretaker was Chris Wiltshire of Bailey Street.

The Club was run on strict disciplinary lines; membership was open to boys over twelve years of age, although I believe Ben Davies and a few tall lads managed it at eleven! The Club attracted members from a wide area and the young people were invited to sit on the committees that ran the various sections.

The Club became famous for the high quality of its team sports, especially at football, gymnastics and basketball. Among those who won the Boys' Club Championship of Wales at basketball were Dick Morris, Tommy Pike, Wilf Jones, George Griffin, Hughie Davies and Tommy Daniels.

The gymnastic teams consisted of Reg Holland, Bill Baker, Bill Gomm, Tommy Daniels, Jack Parker, David Morris, Billy Ward, Tony Evans and many more, with leaders such as Tom Lister, Tom Cowhig and David Jones of Pleasant View.

There was always a strong football interest in the Club, and after the Second World War, Jack Jennings came to the valley to look after the Carpenters Arms in Ynyshir. He had played at full-back for Middlesbrough and at International level for England, and he took over the training of the football team.

He was a strict disciplinarian and held regular training sessions, enforcing a 'no smoking' policy! He also held tactical lessons, using a table to explain his plan of attack and expecting every member of the team to give the same commitment as himself. It was due to this dedication and training that the Boys' Club football team won many cups throughout the South Wales League.

There were more cultural subjects, of course, with a good drama group and singers, led by Sam Jones, and even a debating class began in 1934.

Wattstown Boys Club Football Team, 1929-1930.
Back row: Tom Rawles, Bill Maddern, Dai Williams, Cecil Evans, Dai Benjy Edwards, Alf Phelps.
Front row: Bob Jenkins, Jim Phelps, Tom Rees Edwards, Dai Smith, Mervyn Davey,
Ossie Williams, Bryn Lloyd.

Wattstown Girls at St Athan Camp, c1930s`.
Included in the group are: Valmai Morris, Beryl Maddern, Dilys Cooper, Olwen Rees,
Marie Griffiths, Ida Williams, Bessie Williams, Beryl Johnson, Valerie Thomas.
All the girls wore the club uniform – a blue tunic with a white blouse.

The Girls Club in St Athan, circa 1930s

209

Another group at St Athan.
Valmai Morris third from the left in the front row.

The boys enjoyed themselves, too. Another group in St Athan, circa 1930s

Schoolboys in St Athan, the winners of the Football Shield in 1948. Teacher, Mr Jenkin Williams.

They include: Lawrence Vale, Howard Stewart, Ken Hutchings, John Williams, Arthur Jenkins, Gareth Rees, John Jones, Byron Seldon, Jeffrey Fishlock, Steve Norris, David Thompson, Tommy Richards, Glyn Powell, Mervyn Minton, Islwyn Jones, Eddie Davies, Don Philpott, John Luce, Ivor Rees.

The concert hall was well used with choirs and, concerts of all description, exhibitions of the work of the different sections and, during the war, concerts were given by E.N.S.A.

Dr Bowen of Porth gave music lessons and, in later years, Cliff Gully held art classes. Keep fit classes for ladies were led by Evy Day and Madge Wiltshire.

The village doctor, Ernest Orr, was a keen sportsman and regularly involved himself in the activities of the Boys' Club. He was good at snooker, billiards, and table tennis and often played in the Club and in the Workmen's Institute.

One of the most popular items at the Club was the Tuesday night dance, when the place would be packed and a queue waiting for the doors to open. Entry cost 4d in old money, and the master of ceremonies would be Jerry Murray or Maxie Walters.

The dances remained popular for many years, and throughout the war years servicemen, home on leave, were welcomed at the Club.

Many will remember it as a building that was very cold in winter and hot in the summer, but this didn't seem to discourage anyone and although many names have not been remembered, others like Tommy Rhys Edwards, Dai Benjy, Roy Wilshire, Allan Griffiths, Jack Collins, Trevor and Harold Gully, Ieuan Griffiths, Cyril Thomas, Les Williams, Ossie Williams, David Jarrett, and Glan Daniels are just a few that come to mind.

William Reed, Bailey Street.
Wales Soccer International 1954.
Bill Reed played for Cardiff City Youth after the War, and moved to Brighton in 1950.
In 1953, he joined Ipswich Town and was capped twice for Wales, against Yugoslavia and Scotland, in 1954.

213

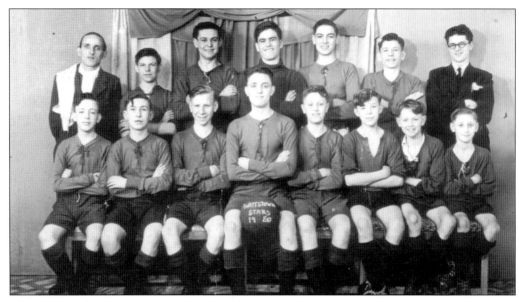

Wattstown Stars Football Club, 1950.
Back row (left to right): Ken Phillips, Ken Hutchings, Ray Robinson, Mal Jones, Tom Richards, John Williams, Bill Dempsey.
Front row: Byron Seldon, John Henley, Ken Jones, John Norris, Steve Norris, Glyn Powell, Colin Roberts, Alec Smith.

Young Miners from various collieries at St Athan Camp in 1952-53.
They include: Lawrence Vale, Iorwerth Matthews, Freddie Griffiths, Elvet Owen, Eddie Griffiths, Tommy Jones, Malcolm Crew, Glyn Martin, Byron Seldon, Raymond Robinson.

214

Ely Valley Cup, 1956-1957.
Back row (left to right): Frank Davies, Merlin Lewis, Mal Crew, Elvet Rossiter, Lance Uzzell.
Middle row: Norman Davies, Alan Jones, Agnes John (Rhondda League Rep),
Arthur Jenkins, George Hopkins
Front row: Byron Seldon, Norman Davies (captain), Roy Lewis, Sammy Syms, Evan Evans,
George Williams.

Owen Morris, Hillside Terrace, photographed in the Forces.
Before the war, he taught Drama in the Boys' Club.
He wrote this poem which tells of the life of the miner.

The hooter blows, its time to rise well before the sun,
Our daily stint in this Rhondda pit is waiting to be done.
We group around the pit head, and huddle to keep warm,
Our face and hands are shining white, but that won't last for long.

The chug-chug of the engine,
The wish-wish of the wheel,
We go down in a soaking cage to a world that's so unreal.
It's a long, long way we have to go to reach the jet black seam,
And each man knows his sweaty job, and does it as a team.

Death is at our elbow, its arrival is not known,
The numerous ways that men are killed is a legend down below.
Maybe the rooftop falls to crush our puny frame,
Or the silent, creeping, unseen death, which bursts with violent flame.

The deep blue scars on face and arms, the sickening, chesty cough,
The slowing down of walking pace, the constant rests and stops.
This is the price that's paid by men to win the jet black coal,
While lying on their stomachs in that dark and dirty hole.

Owen Morris.

216

"Cinderella". On Wednesday and Thursday, the 13th and 14th of January, at the Wattstown Boys` Club, the Ferndale (Christchurch) Dramatic Society under the leadership of the Rev. T. A. Lewis, vicar, gave their second Annual Pantomime, "Cinderella," which was a greater success than last year.

We had to turn a great number away on Wednesday night, owing to lack of room, and on Thursday night the demand for seats was even greater, about 100 persons gathered around the reserved doors long before it started, demanding seats at any price, but as the building was packed to its utmost capacity, they had to go away disappointed.

On Wednesday the Chair was taken by the Rev. T. Jarman of Wattstown and Ynyshir, and on Thursday by L. Phillips, Esq., B.Sc., General Manager.

There was little doubt of the excellence of the show put over by the Society; several well known critics of Pantomime and Drama gave their opinion that with the exception of the scenery, the show was far before that given by professionals at Cardiff and elsewhere.

One of our youngest inhabitants (aged 72 years) came on Wednesday night on a 6d ticket, again on Thursday night on a 1/- ticket and, after the performance, informed the committee she was quite disappointed that the show was not being produced again on Friday!

Our Treasurer could not be found until very late in the evening to hand to him the box-office receipts, but he was eventually discovered by our Limb of the Law, the Colliery Sergeant, wedged up in a corner behind the wings, and when asked to explain his unseemly conduct by joining the performers, he replied; "There is only about one square foot of room in this Hall, and having found it, I am sitting in it".

Great credit must be given to the hard work of the ladies, led by Mrs Phillips of Glenside, and the committee, in providing for such packed houses, and the only complaint they could have had was that they had to turn so many away. Next year we hope to have a larger hall.

Robert Clarke

Robert Clarke kept the garage in Aberllechau Road where the hairdressers stood. He was a keen motorcycle enthusiast and won many trophies for his energetic racing style. A news report of August 7th. 1928 states:

"A beflagged Aberllechau Road today welcomes home Robert Clarke, The Garage, Wattstown, after his great feat at Pendine, where he won the Welsh 100 miles Motor Cycle Race.

The conditions were so bad that only three out of the twenty-five starters completed the course. Mr. Clarke said, 'It was like a dream!' He won on a privately-entered Ariel cycle."

During the 1920s, the people of Wattstown held their carnival in the football ground and Robert Clarke organised competitions and 'gymkhanas' involving motorcycles, where entrants rode around obstacle courses.

His enthusiasm led him to form the Rhondda Fach Motor Cycle Club, with headquarters in the Wattstown Hotel. Through his activities, the members of the club were given a conducted tour of the Ariel works in Birmingham, with tea and a petrol fill-up by the company! The photograph shows the club members and their motorcycles lined up before setting out.

Wattstown Social Club

The Wattstown Social Club, once the National Colliery Offices.

The Wattstown Club Skittles Team.
Back row (left to right): Trevor Morgan, Mervyn Davies, Cyril Greedy, Trevor Gwilym,
Dennis Evans, Emlyn Thomas,
Front row: Allan Jones, George Ward, Albert Down, Ron James, Evan Evans, Iorrie Jones.

The Wattstown Club really began in the Workmen's Institute in 1959, with the assistance of the Fernvale Brewery. In 1965, the Committee felt that new premises were needed, as the old building became unsuitable. The old Colliery Pay Offices became vacant, and they were purchased with a loan from the Brewery. Cameron Brothers of Wattstown were contracted to alter the building by extending the upper floor, and fitting it out as licensed premises. The total cost of this was £54,000. The Club was known officially as The Wattstown Social Welfare Centre, and opened on 3rd August 1965.

The new club began with a change of Committee as follows:

> Chairman: Ron James
>
> Secretary: Dennis Evans
>
> Treasurer: Glyn Powell
>
> The Trustees remained the same.

Others took their places as time passed; Ron Hughes became Secretary and George Ward became a Trustee.

Under the Rules, the Management Committee shall consist of 24 members, 6 ex officio members being Trustees.

15 Representative Members, consisting of:

> 6 from the National Coal Board
>
> 6 from the National Union of Mineworkers
>
> 1 from the Wattstown United Football Club
>
> 1 from the National Association of Old Age Pensioners
>
> 1 from the Gardeners Association.

While the Club was still in the Institute, the Steward was Evan Evans, a position he kept when the Club moved to the new premises in Bailey Street. He later took over the fish and chip shop at 26 Aberllechau Road, with Dilys.

These are the Stewards since the beginning:

> Evan Evans
>
> Megan and Bill Roberts
>
> Audrey and Tom Bailey
>
> Mair and Arthur Davies
>
> Margaret and Elved Jones
>
> Ian and Eunice French.

Road Races were held in Wattstown under the auspices of the Wattstown Sports and Social Club. They were organised by Bernard Baldwin, himself an international athlete. Here we see Stan Eldon on his way to winning the Race, some time in the early 1960s.

Wattstown Jazz Band

Christine Jones, Drum Major of the Caledonians Jazz Band in 1975-79.
This photograph was taken at the World Championships at Porthcawl in 1978.

During the summer of 1971, unknown to her parents, Christine Jones of Pleasant View displayed notices throughout the village of a meeting to be held at her home, with the intention of forming a Jazz Band. Quite a number of people turned up, much to the surprise of her parents! However, a committee was formed, and Albert Uzzell, was appointed as Chairman. He had been the Drum Major of a previous band in the village during the years 1936-39, known as the Wattstown Bell Boys. Harry Dance was their Trainer, who had experience as a member of the Ynyshir Savoy and Cabbage Jazz Band before the War.

Christine's mother, Lynfa Jones, took on the job of Secretary. At the next meeting, they decided to name the new band The Wattstown Toreadors, and also to ask Mrs Orr, the widow of Dr Ernest Orr, to become their President. Their first Drum Major was Kathy Evans. She was followed by Teresa Morgan of Aberllechau Road, who won many trophies as Best Drum Major. In 1976, Christine Jones became their Drum Major, and remained so until they disbanded in 1979.

In late 1972, the Band became founder members of the Rhondda League of Jazz Bands. The League was the inspiration of Cyril Jones, and the membership grew quickly to more than 30 bands. It soon had to be expanded to accept the membership of other bands from Taff Ely, Cynon Valley, and the Vale of Glamorgan. A partnership was then set up with the Bridgend and District League of Jazz Bands, and the South Wales League of Jazz Bands, which became an organisation consisting of 120 bands. During the seven years of competition, the Band won numerous Cups and Trophies, and set a very high standard that many sought to follow. By 1974, the Wattstown Toreadors were at the top of the League, when they won the Rhondda League and the Rhondda/Bridgend Inter-League Championships, taking First Prizes for Best Band, Best Dressed Band, and Best Music, under their trainer Gwyn Green. Their Secretary was Terry Davies of Heol Llechau.

The members were each given a scroll in honour of their achievements, and presented with the Freedom of Wattstown. In all, that year they had won 12 First Prizes in successive weeks, and 40 cups and trophies, while Gwyn Green took First Prize for best Trainer. The Band repeated their successes many times over during the following five years. In 1975, the Band changed its name to Wattstown Caledonians, and were now travelling as far as the West Country and the North of England, to appear in Carnivals, Fairs and Competitions.

They were fortunate to have the services of a professional musician, Bill Collier, who gave them music tuition for one hour per week. In 1976 they appeared on television using the March that Mr Collier had written especially for the Caledonians. Their music was considered to be the best played by any Jazz Band in the country and they were televised by BBC Wales during a practice session. The Band entered the World Jazz Band Championships four times from 1976-79, and were runners-up twice, in 1976 and 1978. Their success was recognised throughout the country, and was due not only to the hard work of the members and the committee, but also to the wonderful support of the parents and people of Wattstown who travelled with the Band to their many venues.

The Wattstown Toreadors 1971-1975. This photograph shows them with their many cups and shields, for the competitions that they won, while Teresa Morgan, of Aberllechau Road, won the title of Best Drum Major many times.

The Wattstown Caledonians Jazz Band, 1975-1979. They entered the World Championships Jazz Band Competitions, and were runners-up in 1975 and 1977. In 1978, they became Triple Crown Winners against the Rhondda, Bridgend, and South Wales Association of Jazz Bands.

Wattstown R.F.C.

The Wattstown Rugby Club, built in 1991 on the site of Danygraig Terrace

Wattstown R.F.C. 1977-78.
Back row (left to right): D. Jones, J. Marden, W. Llewelyn, D. Hopkins, P. Horton, N. Shears, T. Jarvis,
T.Walters, P.Evans.
Middle row: J. Lewis (secretary), R. Lee (president), S. Mardon (captain), M. Clement (chairman),
M. Stevens, T. Williams.
Front row: G. Lee, G. Parsons, M. Coleman, R. James, S. Thomas, J. Harris.

230

Rugby football has been played in Wattstown for almost as long as the village has existed. Although little is known of the early teams, *The Glamorgan Free Press and Rhondda Leader* record that games took place as early as 1898. No names were given but the fact was that a team was in existence over 100 years ago. The players would, have consisted of mainly younger miners from the National Colliery. For them, this meant washing at the end of the shift, and walking to the place where the game was to be played. There was no park in those days and games would take place in a field at the top of Pleasant View, and the teams would change in the Wattstown Hotel when playing at home.

There are records of a Wattstown team playing in the 1920s in the 'Glamorgan League'. The stronger teams in those days were Treorchy, Mountain Ash and Pontypridd, who all played in the same division. On 17th March 1921, Wattstown played Tylorstown away. Wattstown was unable to raise fifteen players, and both teams agreed to play with 12 men only. The following January 1922, Abercarn beat Wattstown 40 points to 3. The Wattstown Boys Club, formed in 1928, had its own rugby team, led by H. Matthews of Ynyshir. Mr Rees, the manager of the Cooperative Shop in Aberllechau Road, used to play, and Mr George Owen of the Wattstown Hotel was a keen instructor, and later became a very able referee.

The present-day Club began in the Wattstown Hotel, where the latest Welsh performance was keenly discussed and dissected during the heady days of the 1970s, when the national team was top of the heap. People like Gerald Lee, Stuart Mardon and Mike Clement would meet on Sunday mornings after the Saturday match, and it was in the Spring of 1976 that the proposed formation of a new rugby team was destined to become the Wattstown Rugby Football Club.

In the beginning, they would play other pub teams, and after a match against 'The Bomb' of Ynyshir, the sides decided to amalgamate, with Ron James, a former Pontypridd player, as Coach, and Stuart Mardon as Captain. A committee was formed at the end of 1976, with Mike Clement as Chairman, and Malcolm Spence as Secretary. The Club moved its base to the Ynyshir Hotel in 1979, where the landlord was John Bevan, the Rugby International from Tylorstown, who trained regularly with the squad. Their Secretary at that time was John Lewis, of Prudential fame.

They moved to the Station Hotel, Ynyshir, in 1981, and remained there until their new clubhouse was built on the site of Danygraig Terrace in 1991. Since their formation, the Club's playing performance has improved year by year, and during the 1990s they have won consistently to reach the semi-finals of the Welsh Brewers Cup.

In 1993, they made it to the final, held in the National Stadium, only to be deprived of a well-deserved win by a controversial injury, time try by their opponents from Swansea.The following year, 1994, saw them finally win the National District Cup against Hartridge High School Old Boys, played at the National Stadium. Over the years, they have maintained their winning performances and thoroughly deserve to achieve their objective of Welsh Rugby Union status. Wattstown Rugby Football Club carry on a long tradition that began in the village over 100 years ago. We wish them every success for the future.

Wattstown R.F.C. 1st Team, 1981-82.
Back row (left to right): John Goldsworthy, Emlyn Cameron, Phil Baker, Tyrone Harris, Kim Harris, Meirion Hughes, Andrew Thomas, Graham Stone,
Greg Davies, John Lewis, Paul Jones.
Middle row: Gerald Lee, Kevin Seldon, Nigel Williams, David Smith, Nigel Shears, John Compton, Dale Williams, Ivor Feehan, Mike Clement.
Seated: Dennis Hughes, Stuart Jones.

CLUB ACHIEVEMENTS
CUP COMPETITIONS

National District Cup

1990-91	Semi Finalists v C.I.A.C.S.	at Rodney Parade
1991-92	Semi Finalists v St Albans	at Maesteg R.F.C
1992-93	Finalists v. Birchgrove	at National Stadium
1993-94	Winners v Hartridge, H.S.O.B.	at National Stadium
1995-96	Finalists v St Albans	at National Stadium
1996-97	Finalists v Cambrian	at National Stadium
2000-01	Semi Finalists v Beaufort	at Merthyr R.F.C.

Keith Jones District Cup

1982-83	Winners v Cefn Coed
1984-85	Finalists v Penallta
1988-89	Finalists v Dowlais
1991-92	Winners v Abercwmboi
1992-93	Winners v Bedlinog
1993-94	Winners v Glyncoch
1997-98	Finalists v Glyncoch
1998-99	Winners v Dowlais
1999-00	Finalists v Glyncoch

Ifor Williams District Cup

1984-85 Winners v Tonyrefail ?nds
1985-86 Winners v Glyncoch

Rhondda Districts Merit Table

1981-82 Runners-Up
1983-84 Winners
1984-85 Winners

League Achievements

1990-91	Runners-Up	Rhondda & East Glamorgan, Division 1.
1991-92	Winners	
1992-93	Winners	
1993-94	Winners	
1994-95	Winners	
1995-96	Winners	
1997-98	Runners-Up	S. A. Brains Premier League
1999-00	Winners	
2000-01	Winners	

Coleman District Cup

1989-90	Finalists	Wattstown 1st XV	v Merthyr 2nds
1993-94	Winners	Wattstown 2nds	v Aberaman 3rds
1995-96	Winners	Wattstown 2nds	v Merthyr 3rds
1996-97	Winners	Wattstown 2nds	v Merthyr 3rds
1999-00	Winners	Wattstown 2nds	v Penallta 2nds

Choirs

The Royal Wattstown Male Voice Choir pictured outside Glenside, circa 1920. The conductor was Dan James.

Wattstown Male Voice Choir outside Glenside, with their conductor, Sam Jones, Pleasant View, circa, 1930s.

The Wattstown Ladies Pensioners Choir, with their conductor Matt Rowlands of Lower Bailey Street, in the 1950s.
Most of the faces are recognisable; only nine are missing from the list.
They are listed from left to right.

Mrs Edwards, Molly Morris, Marie Jones, Enoch, Nicholls, Daniels, Parmee, Phelps, Doris Passey, Kennealy, Susan Morgan, Elsie John, Violet Bailey, Maggie Evans, Griffiths, Adelaide Wiltshire, - - Phelps, John, Rees, Davies, - Morgan, Minnie Holland, Winnie Peel, Davey, Emily Williams, -, Griffiths, Maundrell. Greedy, Simmonds, Maggie Smith, Rowlands, Glyn Phillips (accompanist), Alice Hicks, Matt Rowlands, Saunders, Beal, Morgan, Lloyd.

The Choir in Aberllechau School.

239

The Wattstown Glee Party

The Glee Party members in the Wattstown Social Club

The People who lived here

The life of the village was in the people who lived and worked here, who served the community and played a part in its growth and development. Many of those families have descendants still living here, and remain a part of Wattstown.

We must remember that everyone was from somewhere else. Many came from other parts of Wales, and also from parts of the West Country, such as Somerset, Dorset, Cornwall and Devon. Cwtch was a new community and attracted people to work with the sinking of the pit.

When Watts, Watts took over the colliery in 1884, and built houses for the immigrant workers, people began to arrive in large numbers. Watts already owned other pits in Risca, Monmouthshire, and sent experienced people to work here. As a result, news spread and families came to the new colliery, looking for work.

These are just a few of those who came and have played a part in the life of the village since those early days.

Mr Thomas Bowen

Martha Bowen

Tom Bowen came to the Rhondda in the 1870s and married Martha, from Herefordshire, at Frwd Amos Welsh Baptist Church in Penygraig on July 2nd, 1879. He was born in Radnorshire in 1853, and came to live in Cwtch when the pit was being sunk in 1880. He was one of the founders of Bethel Free Mission in 1905. He became the church secretary, and was always known as Pastor Bowen.

He was active in so many parts of the community, and served on the Works Committee of the Labour Council. He was trustee of the Workmen's Institute and worked in the colliery. He and Martha had five daughters and lived to celebrate their 50th wedding anniversary in July 1929.

He died on October 11th, 1931, aged 78.

Her five daughters,
Beatrice, Annie, Maud, Maggie, Bessie.

243

Mary Williams lived in Hawthorn Cottage, Hillside. She was born in 1875 and was married to Thomas Williams in 1899. These were some of the earliest settlers in Cwtch.

Mary Hannah Williams and her three children, who all died at a young age.

Thomas Thompson of 22 Bailey Street, who married Mary Hannah Williams of 24 Hillside Terrace in 1920. He was in the Essex Regiment during the First World War.

James Seldon and his son John James Seldon in 1902.

Edward Langford, who came to Wattstown from Somerset in the early 1900s

The Barrow Family from Evercreech in Somerset. This family came to Cwtch during the 1890s and were some of the early settlers.
Left to right:
Elizabeth, May, Alice, Edith, Elsie, Hugh.

What a smart chap – Hugh Barrow, senior.

Grandma Morgan and her three children, Joseph, Lillian and Nell, c 1905

Grandfather Morgan.
Father of Joseph Morgan, who became
Mayor of Rhondda.

Joe Morgan and his sisters Violet and Nancy.

John Jones "Check",
checkweigher at the National.

Mrs Ann Jones,
his wife.

In loving Remembrance

A Remembrance Card for Private David Jones, who died in captivity in Bulgaria during the First World War. He was the son of Ann and John Jones "Check".

The Peel family in 1914, when they came to live in Pleasant View.
Left to right: William, Adam, David, Linda, and Winnie. Linda died at 99 in the year 2002.

The Holland family in 1907.
Their parents came from Devon to work in Morriston. Ernest and Minnie married in Morriston and came to Wattstown in 1914.
The boy standing on the chair is Abner Holland, brother of Reginald Holland of Pleasant View, now 94 . The baby on his mother's lap was Vincent, who died aged 5 in 1912.

The Martin family of 56 Hillside Terrace,
c. 1915
Left to right:
Fred, Emily, Will. Frederick, Jane, Emily,
Charlie, Doris, Gladys, Florrie.
Fred Martin took a day off from working
in the pit to go to Barry Island.
Unknowingly, he had saved his own life;
it was the day of the disaster in 1905.
Doris lived in the same house for 91 years
and died in 2002.

Jane Thomas and her son George Thomas
(deaf and dumb, who became the cobbler in
Chapel Street).
Jane later remarried and became Mrs Piper.

The Lovering family: Ronald, Lillian, Doreen, Harry, Edgar and Violet

John, Wyndham and Megan Jones, of
14 Pleasant View, in 1924

Mrs Maud Mills on the day she sat her
midwife examination in Cardiff on April 17th, 1917

Fred 'Bunny' Osborne, of Pleasant View. Fred, as a young man, would spar with other boxers in the Wattstown Hotel. In later years, he was converted and became a member of the Pentecostal Church.

Louise Frederick.
Louise was the daughter of Thomas Frederick, a sailor who worked on a whaling ship. He was a Dominican, and met his future wife Emily, who came from Bristol, when his ship docked at Cardiff. They came to work in Wattstown, but lived for a while in Tylorstown, where Louise was born in 1902. They moved to Wattstown in 1911, to 84 Pleasant View. Louise married Alexander Frank Pearce, who had come to Wattstown from Midsomer Norton in Somerset, to work in the National. He died at the age of 53 with 'dust'.
Louise died in 1997 at the age of 95.

Miss Elunid Morris, in the Land Army at St Clears in 1942.

An outing to Porthcawl

Bethel Chapel Outing to Barry Island, circa, 1940s

Evacuees staying with families in Hillside Terrace during the 1940s
The fair-headed boy on the window sill is David Thompson.

Hillside Terrace Street Party, circa 1950s

V.E. Party on Hillside Terrace in 1945
In fancy dress are Sal Jones, Betty Jenkins, Maud Mills and, to the right, Valmai Morris.

Neighbours outside No 23 and 24 Hillside Terrace
Left to right: Mrs Long, Mrs Sarah Griffiths, Mrs Alice Hicks, Mrs Hannah Thompson, circa, 1930s

*Valmai Morris and her friend Nan Davies,
bus conductresses on the Rhondda buses in 1943*

Enjoying a tea party in Heol Llechau in 1961

A group, mostly sitting, outside Gorwell
Left to right: George Colcombe, George Mortimer, George Morgan, George Ward, Jack Jones, Fred Osborne

Madge Wiltshire and Evelyn Maddern, looking their best, in 1995

I have had great pleasure in compiling this book, and I hope that your enjoyment in reading it will be as great. It cannot possibly contain all that has happened in 120 years. I'm sure that you will find much more that could have been said but, after almost 4 years, it has to be enough for now. I have to move on. Perhaps the next generation will tell their story of Wattstown in the 21st century. The village has changed, just as we have changed; nothing can stop the progress of time, even if we believe it hasn't always been for the better.

Today, we see a cleaner, brighter valley and our lives and homes are no longer victim to coal dust and poverty. Our young people can look forward to a brighter future and we already enjoy the benefits of our society, for which our forefathers fought and struggled to achieve.